The Missing Ending

The Missing Ending

*Rediscovering the
Joy of the Ascension*

Moira Astin

CANTERBURY
PRESS
Norwich

© Moira Astin 2024
First published in 2024 by the Canterbury Press Norwich

Editorial office
3rd Floor, Invicta House
110 Golden Lane
London EC1Y 0TG, UK
www.canterburypress.co.uk

Canterbury Press is an imprint of Hymns Ancient & Modern Ltd
(a registered charity)

Hymns Ancient & Modern® is a registered trademark of
Hymns Ancient & Modern Ltd
13A Hellesdon Park Road, Norwich,
Norfolk NR6 5DR, UK

All rights reserved. No part of this publication may be reproduced,
stored in a retrieval system, or transmitted,
in any form or by any means, electronic, mechanical,
photocopying or otherwise, without the prior permission of
the publisher, Canterbury Press.

Moira Astin has asserted her right under the Copyright, Designs and Patents
Act 1988 to be identified as the Author of this Work

Scripture quotations, unless otherwise marked, are from the New Revised
Standard Version Bible: Anglicized Edition, copyright © 1989, 1995
National Council of the Churches of Christ in the United States of America.
Used by permission. All rights reserved worldwide.
Scripture quotations marked NEB are taken from the New English Bible,
copyright © Cambridge University Press and Oxford University Press 1961,
1970. All rights reserved.

British Library Cataloguing in Publication data

A catalogue record for this book is available
from the British Library

ISBN: 978 1 78622 603 7

Typeset by Regent Typesetting

*To all the students who have inspired me
by their questions.*

With thanks to the Dioceses of Oxford and
Southwark who have supported my teaching ministry
and given me study leave to read and rediscover the
theology of the Ascension.

Contents

Introduction: The Missing Ending?   1

1. The Luke–Acts Passages   3
2. The Background   14
3. The Ascension in the Other Gospels   26
4. The Ascension in Paul's Letters   33
5. The Ascension in 1 Peter, Revelation and Hebrews   44
6. So, What did Happen?   51
7. Why in Heaven did it Happen?   62
8. Why on Earth did it Happen?   73
9. What the First Theologians Wrote about the Ascension   78
10. The Reformation and the Enlightenment: Use and Dismissal of the Ascension   109
11. The Ascension in the Twentieth Century: The Recovery of the Doctrine   117
12. Finding the Missing Ending: The Ascension for Twenty-first-century Christians   139

Bibliography   145
Index of Bible References   147
Index of Authors   151

Introduction

The Missing Ending?

Have you ever bought a book at a jumble sale? There you find all sorts of old tomes, from bird-spotting guides to crime fiction. Some are almost new, others are so well thumbed that pages are becoming detached. How would you feel about a book, which when you turned the last page you found was missing the finale? I expect you'd be frustrated and then would go to find another copy which did have the last page or two, to find out what was written on those final pages. The whole story only comes together when you can see it through from beginning to end. Or perhaps you have bought a second-hand jigsaw only to find the vital piece that makes the picture whole is missing.

Yet today much of the Church seems to have thrown away the last verses of Matthew and Luke's Gospels, where they speak of Jesus' departure from this world, his Ascension. While they are still printed in our Bibles, they are often unread and undervalued. Our theology textbooks focus on the incarnation, when the Son of God became human, and the events of Good Friday when the man who is God died for us, and on the resurrection, but the Ascension is frequently left out as though it's an unimportant doctrine.

This may be because for the last 1,700 years or so the Church has celebrated the Ascension on a Thursday, being the day of the week on which the fortieth day after Easter Sunday falls, the date assigned by Luke in Acts to the final appearance of Jesus to his disciples. It may be that the faithful of previous generations made the effort to attend services on Ascension Day and so to hear the ending of the story of the journey of salvation: the journey of the Son of God to become a human, to be born of Mary, to live and grow, to teach and heal, to die, descend to the dead and then to rise, and to ascend to where he was before, but now taking our humanity into the very presence of God – the journey which together with the work of the Spirit in our lives brings us salvation. Today we often miss out on the ending of this journey.

The feast of Christ the King was introduced in recent years to try and address this deficit, but too often it is seen more as a precursor to Advent, when thoughts of the final judgement are in focus, rather than the ongoing importance of the Ascension of Jesus.

This book aims to make up this deficit, and to show why the Ascension matters, and why it needs to be returned to its place in our teaching and understanding of doctrine.

How to read this book

My initial intention when reading up on the Ascension was to write a short book, to be the extra chapter that seems to be missing from those theology textbooks. If this is what you are looking for it is to be found in Chapters 6, 7 and 8. These cover what the biblical material tells us about what happened at the Ascension and why it happened. If you feel you want a little more, the final chapter outlines the implications of the Ascension for the twenty-first century.

But when I came to write the book it seemed that I needed to explore the texts in more detail, so the first part of this book, from Chapter 1 to Chapter 5, sets the middle chapters in the context of the Bible, including some of the apocryphal books which give the background to the New Testament ideas. The last few chapters before the conclusion give a survey of the major thinkers' writing on the Ascension for those who want to see how understanding has developed over the centuries.

I hope you will enjoy reading the 'missing' ending!

I

The Luke–Acts Passages

If we want to think about the Ascension and what the Bible says about it, the obvious place to start is in the descriptions of it in Luke and Acts. Other books of the Bible refer to or imply the Ascension, but only Luke and Acts describe an event that can be called *the Ascension* as such.

In Luke 24.50–53 and in Acts 1.6–11 Luke[1] describes Jesus' final meeting in physical form with his disciples and his physical departure from them. But before we look at these two versions of the event, it is important to be sure we are looking at what Luke actually wrote.

Which text?

When we open our Bibles and read, we are not reading what Luke actually wrote himself. For a start he wrote in first-century Greek, not in English. So, the text has been translated. But the translators did not have a straightforward task. For when they came to Luke and Acts they had at least two groups of manuscripts they could follow, which in some parts were quite different from each other. Indeed, looking at these texts is a good way of seeing what a complex job the translators have to get us our Bibles in English.

Before printing was invented in the fifteenth century, the only way to have a copy of the Bible was to write it out by hand. The

---

[1] Although the really scholarly and keen will talk of the author of Luke–Acts to show that they can't be sure that it was Luke himself who wrote it, it is simplest just to call him Luke for now. After all, this book is not about who wrote Luke and Acts!

The Missing Ending

monasteries that developed from the fourth century onwards were the main places where copying happened, and the manuscripts that were copied were in several languages. Many were the Latin versions of the Bible, copies of the Vulgate translation of St Jerome, which he first made in the very early fifth century. In other parts of the world the manuscripts were translations of the Greek into Syriac, Coptic, Slavic and other languages, and there are several thousand such manuscripts. These translations are useful other sources of information about what the original text was, but the most important copies for translators are those that are in the Greek of the first century – New Testament Greek as it is now known. The manuscripts all differ a little from one another since they were copied by fallible humans.

When it comes to Luke and Acts there are two main groups of manuscripts, the Alexandrian and the Western texts. The main manuscript in the Western group is the Codex Bezae, a fifth-century manuscript which was in Lyon for much of its existence before being taken by the Protestant scholar Theodore Beza in 1562. He gave it to Cambridge University in 1581 for safe keeping; it is sometimes known as 'D'. The Alexandrian group is represented by the Codex Sinaiticus which was preserved at St Catherine's Monastery in Sinai until the nineteenth century; today, parts of it are to be found in four different places including the British Library. The Western text of Acts is about 10 per cent longer than the Alexandrian text. So we have two different versions of the same books. There are various ideas about why these two versions exist:

(1) The author himself produced two versions of his work. The suggestion is that Luke had written a history of the early Church, the Western text, and subsequently wanted to present it to his friend Theophilus, so he rewrote it for him, polishing the text and taking out things that were superfluous. This gave a slightly shorter version which is preserved in the Alexandrian text.

But why would an author miss out things he thought important before? Also, there are important differences between the two texts. For example, in 21.16 the Western

The Luke–Acts Passages

text records Paul breaking his journey to Jerusalem at the house of Mnason, whereas the Alexandrian text implies Mnason's house is in Jerusalem. Also, the Western text tends to use longer titles for Jesus. For example, in Acts 7.55 in the Alexandrian text Stephen sees Jesus, but in the Western text he sees the *Lord* Jesus. Would Luke really miss out the titles of respect to Jesus that he had given him before?

(2) So another idea is that Luke, when in Rome, had given readings of his work with added explanations, which were copied down by someone else as the second form of the work. After this other people added the extra parts (known as interpolations) in the Western text. There were scribes copying it out in the second and third centuries before the books of the Bible had been fixed: the authoritative list of the New Testament books, known as the *canon*, was only finally decided in the late fourth century.

(3) Perhaps these additions were the work of one reviser in the second century. In this case the idea is that the revision was done to form a version worthy of inclusion in the canon of Scripture which was being developed.

4) But it could be that the Western version is primary and the Alexandrian text was a deliberate revision; there is no reason in the texts to decide which came first after all.

Whatever the reason for the two sets of texts, when a translation is made the translator must decide which to follow, and that is not always easy. In the end most translators decide on a case-by-case basis. But it does matter which text is chosen, since each version has a slightly different theological emphasis.

The Missing Ending

What are the text differences in the accounts of the Ascension?

Both versions of the story, in Luke and in Acts, have significant differences between the two texts. Curiously, at this point the Western form is shorter than the Alexandrian text, even though the Western text is longer in most other places. The New English Bible and the New Revised Standard Version have each based their translation of Luke on a different text group at this point, and so they help us to see the differences between the two.

Verse	Alexandrian form (as translated by the NRSV)	Western form (as translated by the NEB)
Luke 24.51	While he was blessing them, he withdrew from them *and was carried up into heaven.*	... and in the act of blessing them he parted from them.
Luke 24.52	*And they worshipped him* and returned to Jerusalem with great joy	And they returned to Jerusalem with great joy

In Acts there are also differences between the two texts but this does not show up in comparing these two translations. Here instead is a translation of the Western text made in 1923, which shows in brackets the words that are additional in the Alexandrian text.

The Luke–Acts Passages

> **Acts 1.6–11**
> They therefore, when they were come together, asked him, saying, Lord, dost thou at this time restore the kingdom of Israel? And he said unto them, It is not for you to know times or seasons, which the Father hath set within his own authority. But ye shall receive power, when the Holy Spirit is come upon you; and ye shall be my witnesses both in Jerusalem, and in all Judaea and Samaria, and unto the uttermost part of the earth. And when he had said these things, [as they were looking], a cloud received him, and he was taken away out of their sight. And while they were looking steadfastly into heaven as he went, behold, two men stood by them in white apparel; which also said, Ye men of Galilee, why stand ye looking into heaven? This Jesus, which was received up from you [into heaven], shall so come in like manner as ye beheld him going into heaven. (This is a translation of the Western text, done in 1923 by James Wilson, available from http://www.ccel.org/ccel/pearse/morefathers/files/acts_long_02_text.htm.)

Do these differences matter?

The differences matter for two reasons. First, they show a *theological* difference between the two text types. In Luke's Gospel the Western text type, without the extra words, is playing down the *literal* aspects of the Ascension. If this text is followed Jesus departs from the disciples for a final time, rather than being carried up to heaven. The disciples' response is to return to Jerusalem, rather than to worship him. The Alexandrian text is emphasizing something about Jesus – he is in heaven and he is to be worshipped – that the Western text does not highlight at this point. Second, and this is true for the whole of the Bible, we have to be a little careful when we use our English translations: they are only as good as the decisions that have been made by the translators.

How do we decide which text to follow?

It could be argued that we should go with the shorter Alexandrian text since shorter readings are to be preferred to longer readings, unless the omission can clearly be explained by the scribe accidentally skipping a few words. This is the route that is usually chosen by people compiling the texts of the Bible. The idea is that the oldest version is shortest, and as the version is copied extra words are added as comments by the monk doing the work. However, in the 1960s some papyri of part of the New Testament were found which had the longer, Alexandrian form. These papyri, known as the Bodmer Papyri, were dated to the second century, which shows that the Alexandrian version is indeed old. Because of this, most scholars since 1971 have accepted the extra words, and they are translated, often without footnote, in recent versions of the Bible.

This version will be used for the rest of this book, but it is important to be aware that the debate is still live. The Bodmer Papyri do not prove that the Alexandrian text is original – it could still be a second-century revision. So it is important to remember that when we open our Bibles we cannot be absolutely sure that we are reading what was originally written. It is, however, what the contemporary Church agrees to be the most likely text. That will have to suffice us in this imperfect world.

What about the differences in the accounts in Luke and Acts

Having thought about which version of the text to follow, we now look at the text. Luke has described the same event twice but there are differences between his two accounts. To highlight the import points, the key words are in bold, with a letter against the relevant section.

The Luke–Acts Passages

Luke 24.40–53	Acts 1.1–12
And when he had said this, he showed them his hands and his feet.[a] While in their joy they were disbelieving and still wondering, he said to them, 'Have you anything here to eat?' They gave him a piece of broiled fish, and he took it and ate in their presence. Then he said to them, 'These are my words that I spoke to you while I was still with you – that everything written about me in the law of Moses, the prophets, and the psalms must be fulfilled.' Then he opened their minds to understand the scriptures, and he said to them, 'Thus it is written, that the Messiah is to suffer and to rise from the dead on the third day, and that repentance and forgiveness of sins is to be proclaimed in his name to all nations, beginning from Jerusalem. You are witnesses of these things. And see, I am sending upon you what my Father promised; so stay here in the city until you have been clothed with power from on high.'	In the first book, Theophilus, I wrote about all that Jesus did and taught from the beginning until the day when he was taken up to heaven, after giving instructions through the Holy Spirit to the apostles whom he had chosen. After his suffering he presented himself alive to them by many convincing proofs, **appearing to them over the course of forty days**[a] and speaking about the kingdom of God. While staying with them, he ordered them not to leave Jerusalem, but to wait there for the promise of the Father. 'This', he said, 'is what you have heard from me; for John baptized with water, but you will be baptized with the Holy Spirit not many days from now.' So when they had come together, they asked him, 'Lord, is this the time when you will restore the kingdom to Israel?' He replied, 'It is not for you to know the times or periods that the Father has set by his own authority. But you will receive power when the Holy

The Missing Ending

Then[a] he led them out as far as **Bethany**[b], and, **lifting up his hands**[c], he blessed them. While he was blessing them, **he withdrew from them and was carried up into heaven**[d][e]. And they worshipped him, and returned to Jerusalem with great joy; and they were continually **in the temple**[f] blessing God.	Spirit has come upon you; and you will be my witnesses in Jerusalem, in all Judea and Samaria, and to the ends of the earth.' When he had said this, as they were watching, **he was lifted up, and a cloud took him out of their sight. While he was going and they were gazing up towards heaven**[c], **suddenly two men in white robes stood by them. They said, 'Men of Galilee, why do you stand looking up towards heaven? This Jesus, who has been taken up from you into heaven, will come in the same way as you saw him go into heaven.'**[d] Then they returned to Jerusalem from **the mount called Olivet**[b], which is near Jerusalem, a sabbath day's journey away.

(a) The texts differ in when the Ascension happened. In Luke 24.1 we are told that it is the first day of the week and that the tomb has been found empty. We hear of the journey to Emmaus and then the appearance of Jesus to his disciples in Jerusalem. Verse 51 begins with the word 'then', which implies that what follows is on the same day. So, in Luke the Ascension occurs on the evening of the day of the resurrection.

However, in Acts Luke writes of Jesus appearing to the disciples for 40 days before the Ascension.

The Luke–Acts Passages

(b) The location of the Ascension is different in the two accounts: in Luke 24.1 we read that it is Bethany, whereas in Acts 1.12 they return from 'the mount called Olivet'.
(c) In Luke Jesus lifts up his hands to bless his disciples before he ascends; this is not mentioned in Acts.
(d) In Luke there is no description of what happens apart from Jesus being carried up to heaven, while Acts tells us that a cloud hid him from their sight, and that it happened on a mountain.
(e) Luke does not record the appearance of the angels, but the Acts version does. In Luke what the disciples see is sufficient, while in Acts they hear about what has happened as well.
(f) In Acts the disciples return to the upper room and pray, whereas in Luke they are 'continually in the temple', worshipping God.

Why are there these differences?

Luke offers a good example of how we can compare similar passages and learn from them about what the author was trying to do at each point. In most other places in the New Testament we are comparing what was written by one writer with another, and so we cannot be sure that the two knew the same things about the event they are describing. If they didn't, then any difference between what they wrote might have been as much in their sources, whether oral or written, as in their choices about what to write.

But when we compare the book of Luke with the book of Acts we are dealing with the same author, so if there are differences there must be a reason for them.

Some may argue that the reason for the differences is that Luke learned more between writing the Gospel and Acts. This would mean that there were two traditions circulating: in one Jesus ascended on Easter Day; in the other there was a pause of 40 days before he ascended. When Luke heard of this second tradition he corrected his first work by describing the event again with the new information. Looking at other parts of the

The Missing Ending

Bible, particularly John 20, you can see a clear tradition in which Jesus ascended on Easter Day. The tradition of a later Ascension, on the other hand, is repeated in Acts 13.31 where in his sermon Paul says, 'But God raised him from the dead; and for many days he appeared to those who came up with him from Galilee to Jerusalem, and they are now his witnesses to the people.'

However, there is no need to argue that Luke learned more between writing the two works, if we believe that he could describe the same event in different ways because he wants to achieve different things in each place. If we accept that Luke is not tied to a view of history in which every detail has to be made clear at every telling (which is rarely followed even in contemporary history writing), then it is reasonable to believe that Luke was highlighting different aspects of the event for a purpose. Looking at the differences can tell us more about what Luke was trying to do in each place, what mattered to him in each account.

One reason why Luke recounts the event differently in each place is that they form a different part of each book. In Luke's Gospel the account ends the book. Because of this Luke does not want to go into great detail, but prefers to use the account to come full circle on themes in his work. So the Ascension is from Bethany because this is where Jesus started out on his triumphal entry into Jerusalem. He returns to Bethany after his death and resurrection for a triumphal departure. The blessing of his disciples shows Jesus as priestly, and acts as a way of closing the book – just as a blessing closes our worship. The disciples go to the Temple to praise God, and this resolves the tensions with the authorities – for this book at least. The number of days is not important here because Luke is taking a long view. It is a bit as if he is zooming out, and leaving the details light as he artistically closes and sweeps us away from his Gospel, into worship of God with those first disciples.

In Acts, however, Luke has a different purpose. By repeating the event he is linking his two volumes together. But the different details serve to launch his new account. So, Jesus and his disciples are on the Mount of Olives, which reminds the reader that this is where Jesus went to pray, to be close to God. The disciples then go to the upper room to *pray*. The 40 days are included, partly because Luke believed that there had been a period between the resurrection and Jesus' final appearance to his disciples, and to show that the disciples had time for instruction from the resurrected Lord, but also because it is appropriate to have a fuller narrative to begin an account.

Another reason for the differences between Luke and Acts is that Luke has a different theological emphasis in each place. In the Gospel, Jesus blesses the disciples and they return to Jerusalem with joy. This may seem an unusual emotion when someone important has left, but leaves Luke's readers with anticipation of what comes next, not just for the disciples of the account, but for the readers themselves. In Acts, the greater details are present to show Jesus' power and to link Jesus to the gift of the Holy Spirit. In Acts, Luke also emphasizes that the disciples were eye-witnesses. This is important since his book is an account of how these witnesses took what they had seen and told it in Jerusalem, Judea, Samaria and to the ends of the earth.

So, in Luke the Ascension happened on Easter Day and in Acts it occurred 40 days later. But which is true? When did the Ascension happen? To resolve this we need to look at the rest of the Bible, for there we will find the background ideas behind what Luke is saying.

2

The Background

So far we have looked at how we decided which Greek text to follow (known as textual criticism), and at how two versions of the same event can be used to show the theological ideas that the author was wanting to present (known as redactional criticism); but the context of what was being written helps us to understand it further. In this chapter we will look at the background against which Luke was writing – both the ideas and images with which his readers would be familiar, and also what he himself has said earlier in his Gospel which helps us to understand what he means when he writes of the Ascension.

The Old Testament background

Although Luke was a Gentile who was writing to the Gentile Theophilus, it is likely that both were familiar with the Old Testament. They would have been what Luke refers to in Acts as 'God-fearers', Gentiles who were attracted by Judaism and the worship of one God. So when Luke writes of the Ascension he is likely to expect his readers to be aware of this background, and to use it to help them to see what he is describing.

Enoch

In Genesis 5, in the list of Adam's descendants, is the intriguing mention of Enoch. Enoch was Noah's grandfather, and verse 24 tells us that Enoch was no more because God took him away. This was to be picked up by later Jewish writings, but the Bible gives us no more information. Yet the idea of God taking someone to be with him, such that their body is not to be found on earth, is there in this verse.

Elijah

How Elijah was taken up to heaven is the subject of 2 Kings 2. Elijah was a great prophet who had stood up to Ahab and was supported by Elisha. The Bible does not tell us why Elijah was taken up to heaven, merely that this was what happened.

In verses 1–6 we hear Elijah telling Elisha to stay in different places, but Elisha refuses to be parted from his master. In verses 9–10 Elijah promises Elisha a double portion of his spirit (that is, the Spirit of God which is upon him) if he sees him when he is taken. Verse 11 tells of the appearance of a chariot of fire with horses of fire, but Elijah is taken up to heaven in a whirlwind. This does not really give details of what Elisha saw; the emphasis is on God's action and on Elijah being taken up bodily, to go to heaven.

Having seen his master go, Elisha calls on God, and then is able to perform the same parting of the water that Elijah had done, showing that he does indeed have the Spirit on him.

Psalms

When reflecting on the Ascension early Christian writers drew on the Psalms, in particular Psalms 24, 47, 68 and 110.

Scholars have tried to work out what a particular psalm was used for in the life and worship of Israel. This is called the *Sitz im Leben*, a German term since many of those who looked at the Psalms in this way were German; in English that is 'life setting'. One idea is that several of them referred to an annual autumn celebration of Yahweh as Israel's king; these included Psalm 24 and Psalms 47, 68 and 110.

Whether this is a correct interpretation of these psalms or not, they certainly speak of going *up*, and of *God's reign*. So in Psalm 24 we read:

> Who shall ascend the hill of the Lord?
> And who shall stand in his holy place?

So those who are pure may go up to Zion, where God enters, who is glorious and has triumphed in battle. This must be symbolic, since the Old Testament writers knew that God was not to be contained in one place. Hence we may see the psalm as being about a festival in which the Ark comes up the hill to the Temple, there to represent God's reign over Israel and the world.

Psalm 47 describes a procession in which God ascends amid shouts of joy:

> God has gone up with a shout,
> the Lord with the sound of a trumpet

And having gone up, God reigns.

> God is king over the nations;
> God sits on his holy throne.

In Psalm 110 we read:

> The Lord says to my lord,
>   'Sit at my right hand
> until I make your enemies your footstool'
> The Lord sends out from Zion
>   your mighty sceptre
>   Rule in the midst of your foes.

The psalm has in view someone who is reigning on God's behalf – the king in the line of David who was chosen by God to be king over Israel, under God. Interestingly, in this psalm the king is also a priest:

> The Lord has sworn and will not change his mind,
>   'You are a priest for ever according to the order
>   of Melchizedek.'

The Background

Psalm 68 is used by Paul to speak of the Ascension in Ephesians, since it actually refers to ascending on high.

> Why do you look with envy, O many-peaked mountain,
>   at the mount that God desired for his abode,
>   where the LORD will reside for ever?
> With mighty chariotry, twice ten thousand,
>   thousands upon thousands,
>   the Lord came from Sinai into the holy place.
> You ascended the high mount,
>   leading captives in your train
>   and receiving gifts from people,
> even from those who rebel against the LORD God's
>   abiding there.

In the context the ascending referred to is clearly going up Mount Zion, to the Temple, where God reigns.

Daniel 7

The prophet Daniel has been interpreting the dreams of others, but now in his book he tells of his own visions. The first of these is to be found in Daniel 7. In this the prophet sees four monsters coming up out of the sea. Each represents an empire, probably Babylon, the Medes, the Persians and the Greeks. The last monster divides, via its horns, to represent rival kingdoms, as the generals split Alexander the Great's Greek empire after his death.

With this background of human affairs, the prophet says:

> As I watched,
> thrones were set in place,
>   and an Ancient One took his throne;
> his clothing was white as snow,
>   and the hair of his head like pure wool;
> his throne was fiery flames,
>   and its wheels were burning fire.

The Missing Ending

A stream of fire issued,
   and flowed out from his presence.
A thousand thousand served him,
   and ten thousand times ten thousand stood attending him.
The court sat in judgement,
   and the books were opened.
I watched then because of the noise of the arrogant words that the horn was speaking. And as I watched, the beast was put to death, and its body destroyed and given over to be burned with fire. As for the rest of the beasts, their dominion was taken away, but their lives were prolonged for a season and a time. As I watched in the night visions,
I saw one like a human being
   coming with the clouds of heaven.
And he came to the Ancient One
   and was presented before him
To him was given dominion
   and glory and kingship,
that all peoples, nations, and languages
   should serve him.
His dominion is an everlasting dominion
   that shall not pass away,
And his kingship is one
   that shall never be destroyed.

This is a picture of a triumphal coming of one 'like a human being', coming on clouds to the Ancient of Days to receive the authority to rule the earth.

   The Old Testament has three themes that would be in the minds of Luke's readers: first, that of the exceptionally righteous person being taken up to heaven bodily; second, that of God and his representative going up to Zion and reigning there; and last, the coming of one 'like a human being' on the clouds of heaven to the Ancient of Days to receive all authority to rule the earth.

The Background

Anabaino

Another aspect of the Old Testament background is the Greek word *anabaino*. This word is used in the Greek version of the Old Testament which is called the Septuagint, the version with which Luke would have been familiar. The word is used in three of these psalms, in Psalm 24, Psalm 47 and Psalm 68, and is translated there as 'ascend'. In the Septuagint the word is used in many other places. It is used of going up on to a roof (Joshua 2.8), or getting up into a chariot (2 Chronicles 10.18), going up to a high place (2 Samuel 15.30), and often of going up to the Temple (e.g., 2 Kings 20.8; 2 Kings 23.2; 2 Chronicles 29.20; Isaiah 38.22; Micah 4.2). From this physical sense, there came a metaphorical use: thus, to say the cry of the Israelites went up to God (Exodus 2.23), *anabaino* is used. It is also used of the cloud going up from the tabernacle (Exodus 40.36, 37; Numbers 9.17, 21), and for the return of God to heaven after his visit to Abraham (Genesis 17.22). Angels also ascend, *anabaino*, to heaven after they have finished their allotted tasks on earth (Genesis 28.12; Judges 13.20).

This word is the one that Luke and other New Testament writers use for Jesus' Ascension.

The inter-testamental books

To us, the books that were written after Malachi and before Jesus seem distant and obscure. We do not read them regularly, if at all. Some of them are printed in some versions of the Bible – they are the Apocrypha. These books were part of the Septuagint, but no Hebrew manuscripts of these works were to be found in the sixteenth century, when Protestants were anxious to get back to the sources of the Bible, turning their backs on later translations. These books, which had been accepted as part of the Bible for centuries before, were regarded as useful, but not now considered to be part of the 'canon' of Scripture, that is, the books that are accepted as inspired by God. Not all inter-testamental books are in the Apocrypha, but all were valued by a group of Jews or Christians at one time or another and are to be distinguished from works of other sects such as the Gnostics, whose books have never been seen as of value to Christians.

How wide a circulation these books had we can't be sure, but those in the Apocrypha would have been familiar to Luke's audience, since they were seen as part of the Jewish scriptures, even if we cannot be so sure of the others.

Tobit (in the Apocrypha)

If you read Tobit 12 you will see that it has the same ingredients as Luke 24, but not in the same order. In Tobit, Raphael the archangel has come from God to help Tobit and his son Tobias. He is now ready to reveal who he is before he returns to heaven.

> 'I will now declare the whole truth to you and will conceal nothing from you. Already I have declared it to you when I said, "It is good to conceal the secret of a king, but to reveal with due honour the works of God." So now, when you and Sarah prayed, it was I who brought and read the record of your prayer before the glory of the Lord, and likewise whenever you buried the dead. And that time when you did not hesitate to get up and leave your dinner to go and bury the dead, I was sent to you to test you. And at the same time God sent me to heal you and Sarah your daughter-in-law. I am Raphael, one of the seven angels who stand ready and enter before the glory of the Lord.'
> The two of them were shaken; they fell face down, for they were afraid. But he said to them, 'Do not be afraid; peace be with you. Bless God for evermore. As for me, when I was with you, I was not acting on my own will, but by the will of God. Bless him each and every day; sing his praises. Although you were watching me, I really did not eat or drink anything – but what you saw was a vision. So now get up from the ground, and acknowledge God. See, I am ascending to him who sent me. Write down all these things that have happened to you.'
> And he ascended. Then they stood up, and could see him no

more. They kept blessing God and singing his praises, and they acknowledged God for these marvellous deeds of his, when an angel of God had appeared to them.
(Tobit 12.11–22)

The account has women taking care of the dead, frightened followers, someone not being seen for who he really is, the blessing of peace being given, and the one ascending and being seen no more. Following this, those who saw it praise God. All these features are found in Luke 24, so perhaps Tobit 12 was in Luke's mind when he wrote his account in his Gospel. Even if it wasn't consciously so, there are certainly echoes of Tobit in what Luke writes.

Sirach or Ecclesiasticus 48 (in the Apocrypha)

Ecclesiasticus (or Sirach, or the Wisdom of Ben Sira, it goes by all three names) is probably a second-century BC work. Ecclesiasticus 44—50 is a hymn in honour of the famous men of the Bible. In chapter 48 it says of Elijah:

> You were taken up by a whirlwind of fire,
>   in a chariot with horses of fire.
> At the appointed time, it is written, you are destined
>   to calm the wrath of God before it breaks out in fury,
> to turn the hearts of parents to their children,
>   and to restore the tribes of Jacob.
> Happy are those who saw you
>   and were adorned with your love!
>   For we also shall surely live.
> When Elijah was enveloped in the whirlwind,
>   Elisha was filled with his spirit.
> He performed twice as many signs,
>   and marvels with every utterance of his mouth.
> Never in his lifetime did he tremble before any ruler,
>   nor could anyone intimidate him at all.
> (Ecclesiasticus 48.9–12)

This picks up the same themes as the book of Kings in Elijah's ascension, the chariot of fire and the whirlwind, with Elisha receiving the spirit, but says it all more poetically.

1 Enoch 62

The First Book of Enoch was probably written in the third century BC. It was well known to the Qumran Community who kept their scrolls in a cave, and these are today known as the Dead Sea Scrolls. It is referred to in Jude, but was not accepted by Rabbinic Judaism as orthodox. The book presents itself as the visions of Enoch the grandfather of Noah, and explores subjects such as the origins of demons and the future judgement of humanity.

> And the righteous and elect shall be saved on that day,
> And they shall never thenceforward see the face of the
>   sinners and unrighteous.
> And the Lord of Spirits will abide over them,
> And with that Son of Man shall they eat
> And lie down and rise up for ever and ever.
> And the righteous and elect shall have risen from the earth,
> And ceased to be of downcast countenance.
> And they shall have been clothed with garments of glory,
> And these shall be the garments of life from the Lord
>   of Spirits:
> And your garments shall not grow old,
> Nor your glory pass away before the Lord of Spirits.

Rising from the earth, whether it is seen as resurrection or ascension, is associated with glory in 1 Enoch 62.

These writings were much better known in Luke's day and may have influenced him when he came to write about what had happened.

The Background

The background in the Gospel of Luke

Luke himself provides a pointer to the Ascension in his account of the Transfiguration. If the book were to be read at one sitting it is likely that the hearers would still have this event in their minds when they come to the final event of the book.

There are many similarities in the account Luke gives in Luke 9.28–36 and the description of the Ascension that Luke gives in Acts 1. If we put them side by side this becomes clear:

Luke 9.28–36	Acts 1.6–12
Now about eight days **after these sayings**[c] **Jesus took with him Peter and John and James**[b], and went up on **the mountain**[a] to pray. And while he was praying, the appearance of his face changed, and his clothes became dazzling white. Suddenly they saw two men, **Moses and Elijah**[e], talking to him. They appeared in glory and were speaking of **his departure**[f], which he was about to accomplish at **Jerusalem**[g]. Now Peter and his companions were weighed down with sleep; but since they had stayed awake, they saw his glory and the two men who stood with him. Just as they were leaving him, Peter said to Jesus, 'Master, it is good for us to be here; let us make three dwellings, one for you,	So **when they had come together**[b], they asked him, 'Lord, is this the time when you will restore the kingdom to Israel?' He replied, 'It is not for you to know the times or periods that the Father has set by his own authority. But you will receive power when the Holy Spirit has come upon you; and you will be my witnesses in Jerusalem, in all Judea and Samaria, and to the ends of the earth.' **When he had said this**[c], as they were watching, he was lifted up, **and a cloud**[d] took him out of their sight. While he was going and they were gazing up towards heaven, suddenly two men in white robes stood by them. They said, 'Men of Galilee, why do you stand looking

one for Moses, and one for Elijah' – not knowing what he said. While he was saying this, **a cloud**^(d) came and overshadowed them; and they were terrified as they entered the cloud. Then from the cloud came a voice that said, 'This is my Son, my Chosen; listen to him!' When the voice had spoken, Jesus was found alone. And they kept silent and in those days told no one any of the things they had seen.	up towards heaven? This Jesus, who has been taken up from you into heaven, will come in the same way as you saw him go into heaven.' Then they returned to Jerusalem from **the mount** ^(a) called Olivet, which is **near Jerusalem**^(g), a sabbath day's journey away.

(a) Both the Transfiguration and the Ascension take place on a mountain. Jesus regularly prayed on the Mount of Olives when he was near Jerusalem – the Garden of Gethsemane is on its slopes. Mountains are significant in the Bible: the law was given to Moses on Mount Sinai; Elijah defeated the prophets of Baal on Mount Carmel, and met with God on Mount Horeb; and the psalms we have looked at all involved going up to Mount Zion, to the Temple.
(b) Jesus is with his disciples on the mountain, both at the Transfiguration and at the Ascension.
(c) In both the event happens after Jesus has been teaching the disciples, so in some ways it is to be seen as an event which is also teaching them.
(d) In both events the cloud that is associated with God's glory is present.
(e) Moses and Elijah are on the mountain with Jesus at the Transfiguration. Both were believed by first-century Jews to have been taken to heaven bodily (this is called 'assumption'). We have looked at Elijah going into heaven above.

The Background

His assumption is also written about in Tobit and Ecclesiasticus. Moses' death is written about in Deuteronomy 34, but Deuteronomy 34.6 says that although he was buried no one knows where his grave is, and so the tradition grew that he had been taken to heaven bodily. A book which is called *The Assumption of Moses* was written in the first century AD and is quoted by Jude in Jude 9.

(f) Jesus' 'departure' is what the discussion on the mountain is about. The Greek word here is *exodos*. Many commentators see in the use of the word *exodos* a reference to Jesus' death and resurrection and the release from slavery to death and sin that they would bring. Without denying that link, it seems reasonable to see Luke as using the word for what it naturally means – Jesus' departure, that is, his Ascension. This can be backed up by the fact that in Acts 13.24 Luke uses the word *eisodos* of Christ's coming into the world. (In Greek *eis* means 'into', and *ex* means 'out of', so *eisodos* means to come into somewhere and *exodos* means to go out of somewhere).

(g) Luke 9 says Jesus' departure will be accomplished at Jerusalem, while in Acts 1.12 Luke draws attention to the fact that the Mount of Olives was near Jerusalem, within a Sabbath day's walk. The importance of this was that anywhere within a Sabbath day's walk could be seen as being at the place itself.

Other aspects of the account suggest that the Transfiguration is connected to the Ascension. For example, in Luke 9.28 we read that Jesus and his disciples went up (*anabaino*) the mountain – the same word that Luke later uses for the Ascension. In Luke 9.51, just a few verses after this account, we are told that 'the days drew near for him to be taken up'. Then Jesus starts his journey to Jerusalem, a journey that will end in his death, resurrection and Ascension – he will be taken up to heaven.

So, when we come to read the account of the Ascension in Luke, we should hear this account of Jesus being seen in his glory and endorsed by his Father as part of the background to what happens.

3

The Ascension in the Other Gospels

Although Luke's accounts of the Ascension are the best known, there are references in the other Gospels. Some of these are more explicit than others, but all help us to piece together more of what the Bible says about the Ascension.

John

Although John does not describe the Ascension he refers to it in two ways. One is in the teaching Jesus gives, which includes references to his going up to heaven. The second is in what he says and does after his resurrection.

John 3

A key theme of John's Gospel is the journey of the Son of God from the eternal to the world of time and back to the eternal by way of the cross. So, when Jesus is in discussion with Nicodemus we read:

> Jesus answered him, 'Are you a teacher of Israel, and yet you do not understand these things? Very truly, I tell you, we speak of what we know and testify to what we have seen; yet you do not receive our testimony. If I have told you about earthly things and you do not believe, how can you believe if I tell you about heavenly things? No one has ascended into heaven except the one who descended from heaven, the Son of Man.

And just as Moses lifted up the serpent in the wilderness, so must the Son of Man be lifted up, that whoever believes in him may have eternal life.' (John 3.10–15)

Jesus is rejecting the claims of other teachers to have gone up to heaven to get special knowledge to then teach others. He alone has been in heaven, and he is the one who has come down, who has descended to the depths of being a human, to the point of death, so that he might return to heaven and take humanity with him. Only the one who has come down from heaven and is willing to do this for us is a worthy teacher, not those who claim special knowledge but cannot show, by the way they live or do the special works of God that Jesus does, the authority for what they teach.

John 6

When many of his disciples heard it, they said, 'This teaching is difficult; who can accept it?' But Jesus, being aware that his disciples were complaining about it, said to them, 'Does this offend you? Then what if you were to see the Son of Man ascending to where he was before? (John 6.60–62)

Jesus has fed the 5,000 with a small boy's provisions of five loaves and two fish (vv. 1–13). The next day he teaches the people that he is the bread of life (v. 35), the bread from heaven (v. 32). In verse 51 he says, 'I am the living bread that came down from heaven. Whoever eats of this bread will live for ever; and the bread that I will give for the life of the world is my flesh.'

As in John 3 we have the theme of Jesus having come down from heaven and returning there. His Ascension and exaltation will make it clear that his teaching is true, and his offering of himself as the bread from heaven will give his followers the life he claims for it.

So, we see Jesus pointing forward to his Ascension as the confirmation of his teaching.

John 16

The evening before his death, Jesus is still teaching his disciples. In chapter 16 he teaches them of the Advocate who will come to them, to help them:

> But now I am going to him who sent me; yet none of you asks me, 'Where are you going?' But because I have said these things to you, sorrow has filled your hearts. Nevertheless, I tell you the truth: it is to your advantage that I go away, for if I do not go away, the Advocate will not come to you; but if I go, I will send him to you. (John 16.5–7)

Here Jesus makes a clear link between his Ascension and the coming of the Holy Spirit. It will be his physical departure from his disciples that will enable the Holy Spirit to come to them. Unless he goes away, the Advocate will not come. But when he has gone to the Father he will send the Holy Spirit to them. This connection is particularly important as we look at what Jesus says after the resurrection.

John 20

In John 20 we read of what happened on the first day of the week, after Jesus has died. The women have found the tomb empty, and when the others have left, Mary is weeping in the garden. There she sees Jesus, who she does not at first recognize. Then we read:

> Jesus said to her, 'Mary!' She turned and said to him in Hebrew, 'Rabbouni!' (which means Teacher). Jesus said to her, 'Do not hold on to me, because I have not yet ascended to the Father. But go to my brothers and say to them, "I am ascending to my Father and your Father, to my God and your God."' (John 20.16–17)

Jesus stops Mary from clinging to him, since he has yet to ascend to his Father. Then he tells her to take a message to his brothers. Interestingly Jesus uses the present tense of *anabaino*: he is ascending, not will ascend, but is ascending now, as she gives the message.

That evening Jesus appears to the disciples, coming to them despite the locked doors. Having greeted them, and shown his hands and side, he says, '"Peace be with you. As the Father has sent me, so I send you." When he had said this, he breathed on them and said to them, "Receive the Holy Spirit"' (John 20.21–22).

So now Jesus gives them the Holy Spirit. But just a few days before Jesus had said that the Holy Spirit would come after he had gone away to the Father, for he can only send the Holy Spirit from the Father.

So while John does not describe the Ascension, any more than he described the resurrection, he tells of the results. Jesus comes to his disciples no longer bound by the physical world – he can go through locked doors. He can give them the Holy Spirit.

Matthew

Matthew does not describe the Ascension either. But we find some references that point to it.

Jesus' Baptism

> And when Jesus had been baptized, just as he came up from the water, suddenly the heavens were opened to him and he saw the Spirit of God descending like a dove and alighting on him. And a voice from heaven said, 'This is my Son, the Beloved, with whom I am well pleased.' (Matthew 3.16–17)

By looking at how this differs from Mark's version we can see that Matthew may be using it as a hint towards the Ascension. For when Jesus has been baptized, where Mark says that Jesus saw the heavens torn apart (Mark 1.10), Matthew says that 'the heavens were opened to him'. So instead of the heavens being opened for the Spirit to come down, in Matthew the heavens are opened to Jesus. We have a pointer to Jesus as the one who is the link between heaven and earth in his humanity, being blessed by God and heaven being open to him.

The Parable of the Talents, Matthew 25

In this tale, the merchant is an allegory of Christ, whose Ascension is the journey to a far country and whose return is expected, although its timing is unknown. This story is thus speaking to Matthew's readers as they are listening to his words, between Jesus' Ascension and his return.

The Trial

At the end of the trial before the High Priest, Jesus says something that seals his fate.

> But Jesus was silent. Then the high priest said to him, 'I put you under oath before the living God, tell us if you are the Messiah, the Son of God.' Jesus said to him, 'You have said so. But I tell you,
> From now on you will see the Son of Man
> seated at the right hand of Power
> and coming on the clouds of heaven.'
> Then the high priest tore his clothes and said, 'He has blasphemed! Why do we still need witnesses? You have now heard his blasphemy.' (Matthew 26.63–65)

'One like a Son of Man', in Daniel 7, came to the Ancient of Days on the clouds of heaven. This is the heavenward side of the Ascension. Where Jesus is no longer seen on earth, the prophet foresees his coming to God in heaven. Jesus' use of this quotation is a claim to be the person God has chosen as his Messiah, who will reign for ever on his behalf, by coming on the clouds of heaven to God. No wonder the High Priest reacted to this claim of supreme authority over humans!

The Final Words of Jesus

Matthew does not recount the Ascension, but he does have a similar scene at the end of his Gospel.

> Now the eleven disciples went to Galilee, to the mountain to which Jesus had directed them. When they saw him, they worshipped him; but some doubted. And Jesus came and said to them, 'All authority in heaven and on earth has been given to me. Go therefore and make disciples of all nations, baptizing them in the name of the Father and of the Son and of the Holy Spirit, and teaching them to obey everything that I have commanded you. And remember, I am with you always, to the end of the age.' (Matthew 28.16–20)

Just as in Luke's Gospel account of the Ascension the disciples are with Jesus on a mountain, and they worship him. But in Luke they worship Jesus after he has left them and been taken into heaven, whereas Matthew shows the disciples worshipping Jesus in his presence. Another difference is that this scene in Matthew happens in Galilee, rather than in Jerusalem.

Matthew then tells the disciples that he has been given all authority. This is the key to seeing why this scene is different from Luke. Luke is telling the human side of the Ascension, of Jesus leaving the earth to return to heaven where he will receive his authority to rule. For Matthew Jesus has already been given authority. In saying that he has been given authority Jesus quotes Daniel 7.14 pretty much word for word. In Daniel, the 'one like a son of man' receives authority after he has come on the clouds of heaven to the Ancient of Days, that is, after his ascent into heaven. So for Matthew Jesus has already ascended to be given his authority and now has returned to send his followers out to act on it.

Just as in John, Matthew tells of the results of the Ascension rather than describing the event, which has occurred prior to the last time that Jesus' followers see him.

Mark

Mark's Gospel in the form that is accepted as original does not mention the Ascension. Most Bibles now make clear that Mark 16.8 is the last part of the book that is from the original author. But the longer ending, which is a second-century addition, does include this verse: 'So then the Lord Jesus, after he had spoken to them, was taken up into heaven and sat down at the right hand of God' (Mark 16.19).

This looks like a summary of Luke's accounts of the Ascension; the author of this longer ending of Mark clearly felt that the work was not complete without adding the Ascension as well as post-resurrection appearances of Jesus.

The Ascension in the Gospels

Both Matthew and John refer to the Ascension. John sees it as something that happened privately on Easter Day, after the resurrection and one meeting of the risen Jesus with Mary, but before the majority of Jesus' appearances to his disciples. Because of his Ascension, Jesus can give the Holy Spirit to his disciples, but he continues to meet with them for some weeks, before they no longer see him physically and must rely on the Holy Spirit to guide them.

Matthew does tell of a final appearance of Jesus to his disciples; it happens in Galilee, and Jesus says he has been given all authority, which implies that he has already appeared before God to be given this authority, as the 'Son of Man'.

Luke tells his account briefly and is relating the *departure* of Jesus. He sets the scene on the late evening of Easter Day. Jesus goes with his disciples to Bethany where, blessing his disciples, he withdraws to heaven. They respond with joy, an unusual reaction to the departure of someone who has been very important to them. This itself is a sign that this is no ordinary departure, but one 'accompanied by his blessing, the undoubted assurance of his abiding presence always in time and for eternity' (Donne, 1983, p. 6).

4

The Ascension in Paul's Letters

Paul is the first pastoral theologian of the Church. He had been involved in the early stages of many churches and writes to them to help them in their development. In some of his letters, such as the early chapters of Romans, he is attempting to set out what he believes in an ordered way, but mostly he is dealing with issues that have arisen in the churches, and his responses draw on what he has discovered of God, through Jesus and the Holy Spirit, to resolve the issue.

So we do not read in Paul a systematic worked-out theology of the Ascension. Rather, it is referred to or assumed as the basis of something else that Paul is interested in. However, these references can be pieced together to give a picture of where Jesus went when he ascended and what he is doing there.

Paul tells us of the Ascension in two ways. On occasion he refers to the event, or to Jesus ascending. Mostly he refers to the *results* of the Ascension – that Jesus is exalted, at the right hand of God the Father – without telling us how he got there. To understand the importance of the Ascension it is necessary to consider both groups of references. But before we look at these there is one other event that has an impact on our understanding of the Ascension, and that is Paul's vision of Jesus.

Paul's vision of Jesus

This is most famously described by Luke in Acts 9, but Paul himself refers to it in 1 Corinthians 15.5–8 and Galatians 1.16.

In Galatians 1 Paul is making it clear to the Galatians that his knowledge of the good news has come to him from God directly rather than second hand. He tells of his life in Judaism, being 'zealous for the traditions of my ancestors' (Galatians 1.14), and continues: 'But when God, who had set me apart before I was born and called me through his grace, was pleased to reveal his Son to me, so that I might proclaim him among the Gentiles, I did not confer with any human being ...' (Galatians 1.15–16).

Paul does not give any details of seeing Jesus but says that it was God who was the one who revealed his Son to him.

In 1 Corinthians 15 Paul is giving the evidence that Jesus has risen from the dead. This is that Jesus who

> ... appeared to Cephas, then to the twelve. Then he appeared to more than five hundred brothers and sisters at one time, most of whom are still alive, though some have died. Then he appeared to James, then to all the apostles. Last of all, as to someone untimely born, he appeared also to me.

Paul here makes no distinction between his meeting with Jesus and those of the other apostles. There is no sense of his meeting being a vision and theirs being physical, there is no distinction at all. Yet Paul clearly met with Jesus after the Ascension as described by Luke in Acts 1.

References to the Ascension

It might be argued that Paul doesn't really know about the Ascension since he does not distinguish between his meeting with Jesus and the meetings that the other apostles had with him. However, Paul does refer to the Ascension in his letters, so clearly he did know about it. For him his meeting Jesus was as real, as valid, even though it clearly took place after the Ascension, as the apostles' meeting with him after the resurrection. In three places he refers to it directly; elsewhere it is the background to the theological ideas about Christ that Paul has in view.

Ephesians 4.7–10

> But each of us was given grace according to the measure of Christ's gift. Therefore it is said,
> 'When he ascended on high he made captivity itself
>   a captive;
>   he gave gifts to his people.'
> (When it says, 'He ascended', what does it mean but that he had also descended into the lower parts of the earth? He who descended is the same one who ascended far above all the heavens, so that he might fill all things.)

In the chapter on the background to the Ascension we saw that Psalm 68 was used by the early Church to help them think about the Ascension. Paul leads the way in this passage. Interestingly, though, he has changed the psalm somewhat. For the psalm says:

> You ascended the high mount,
>   leading captives in your train
>   and receiving gifts from people,
> even from those who rebel against the LORD God's abiding
>   there. (Psalm 68.18)

The picture in the psalm is of God ascending, taking with him tributes of those he has conquered. Paul sees this as referring to Jesus ascending to God, but instead of taking gifts from us to God, his triumph is such that he *gives* gifts, the gifts of the Holy Spirit. So, for Paul the Ascension and the giving of the gifts of the Spirit go hand in hand.

Philippians 2.6–11

> ... who, though he was in the form of God,
>   did not regard equality with God
>   as something to be exploited,
> but emptied himself,
>   taking the form of a slave,
>   being born in human likeness.

And being found in human form,
  he humbled himself
  and became obedient to the point of death –
  even death on a cross.

Therefore God also highly exalted him
  and gave him the name
  that is above every name,
so that at the name of Jesus
  every knee should bend,
  in heaven and on earth and under the earth,
and every tongue should confess
  that Jesus Christ is Lord,
  to the glory of God the Father. (Philippians 2.6–11)

Paul is probably quoting a hymn that is already used in the church. However, he clearly agrees with it and uses it to make his point. In this hymn there is a clear outline of Jesus' journey from 'up' in heaven, 'down' to earth, and 'down' to the cross, and then 'up', being exalted. In fact, the hymn says more than that he is exalted: he is highly exalted – the Greek word used here is *hyperypsosen*. The first part of the word *hyper* is still used in English to mean way more than can be expected normally. So 'God extremely exalted him' would be a better translation, beyond all expectations.

When did this happen? Paul doesn't actually make it clear. It could have been at Jesus' resurrection, and certainly the resurrection was the start, but the 'V'-like journey of the passage begins and ends in heaven, and so the Ascension is clearly in view here.

So, God 'extremely exalted' Jesus, and gave him a name above all other names, that 'every tongue should confess that Jesus Christ is Lord'. It is at his Ascension that Jesus is elevated to the status of Lord. This is the heart of Paul's devotion, not to a human who once lived, but to Jesus the human who is Lord; and by the power of the Spirit we are enabled to call Jesus Lord – no one can say 'Jesus is Lord' except by the Holy Spirit (1 Corinthians 12.3b). This was the one whom Paul met on the road to Damascus, according to Luke: 'He asked, "Who are you, Lord?" The reply came, "I am Jesus, whom you are persecuting"' (Acts 9.5).

1 Timothy 3.16

> Without any doubt, the mystery of our religion is great:
> He was revealed in flesh,
>   vindicated in spirit,
>   seen by angels,
> proclaimed among Gentiles,
>   believed in throughout the world,
>   taken up in glory.

In this passage Paul is using a hymn or creed to guide Timothy in his teaching. The section stands out from the rest of the letter in its style, and it could well be a hymn that was in circulation already. As in the hymn used in Philippians there is no mention of the resurrection as such, indeed in this case the cross is not mentioned either. What is said is that Jesus was 'taken up in glory'.

Interpreting this short passage is not entirely straightforward. At first sight, the last line 'taken up in glory' is about the Ascension; but how does it come about that it is after Jesus' being preached in the world, which clearly is still going on?

To resolve this, it is better to see the passage as falling into two parts or verses. The first three lines are about Jesus on earth, so 'vindicated in spirit' refers either to his miracles or to the greatest miracle of all, the resurrection. Being 'seen by angels' could then be a reference to the Ascension.

The second set of lines are an echo of the first, each line reflecting the idea of the equivalent line in the first set but moving it on beyond the resurrection and Ascension, into how these events have affected the world.

So the Jesus who was revealed in flesh is still being revealed in the proclamation to the Gentiles; Jesus was 'vindicated in spirit', and is still being vindicated by being believed in throughout the world; Jesus was seen by angels at his Ascension, and it was a taking up in glory, which is not the end of the story but moves it into this new phase.

If this is the right way to read the passage, then the reigning of Jesus in glory is what enables Jesus' being proclaimed and being believed in. As he is in glory, his Church is growing on earth. So his being in glory is not about a rest from his labours, but about his renewed work, in the world.

Results of the Ascension

In these verses Paul does not mention Jesus' Ascension, but he is assuming it – for how else could he talk of Jesus being in heaven, unless he understands that the human whom he had probably seen in his life on earth has been taken into heaven?

Romans 8.34

> Who is to condemn? It is Christ Jesus, who died, yes, who was raised, who is at the right hand of God, who indeed intercedes for us.

Jesus is not just in heaven but is at the right hand of God. This is not so much a physical position as the position of one who is sharing in God's glory and reign. It echoes Psalm 110.1, which is about the Davidic king being given God's authority to reign over his people. So Jesus ascended is also Jesus enthroned as the human king who reigns on God's behalf. (This does not deny that Jesus is, and always has been, God the Son).

What does this reigning king do with his power and authority? He intercedes for us with God. This is not the intercession of one begging a disapproving monarch for mercy; it is the bringing of himself and all he has been, as God and as human in his life on earth, before God the Father. In heaven the work of reconciling humans to God is happening now, because of all Jesus achieved on earth. This idea is worked out at much greater length in the book of Hebrews.

The Ascension in Paul's Letters

1 Corinthians 15.23–25

> But each in his own order: Christ the first fruits, then at his coming those who belong to Christ. Then comes the end, when he hands over the kingdom to God the Father, after he has destroyed every ruler and every authority and power. For he must reign until he has put all his enemies under his feet.

In this part of 1 Corinthians Paul is teaching the Corinthians about the resurrection of God's people. He is looking forward to the end of the current in-between time. At the time of Jesus many Jews were expecting that God's people would be resurrected at the end of time, This is seen in Martha's responses to Jesus in John 11.24: 'Martha said to him, "I know that he will rise again in the resurrection on the last day."' In Jesus the resurrection has already begun but is not concluded. So, we are living after the *start* of the end of time, but before the *end* of the end of time. This in-between time is the time of the Church, when, in a sense, we are raised with Jesus, but not raised in our own bodies.

What is Christ doing in this time? He is reigning, until he has put all his enemies under his feet – the last of these will be death itself, when we will be raised into our own new bodies.

So again Jesus' Ascension is the way he got to heaven, and there he is actively reigning, and so involved in what happens on earth.

Ephesians 1.20–23

> God put this power to work in Christ when he raised him from the dead and seated him at his right hand in the heavenly places, far above all rule and authority and power and dominion, and above every name that is named, not only in this age but also in the age to come. And he has put all things under his feet and has made him the head over all things for the church, which is his body, the fullness of him who fills all in all.

This is another place where Paul runs the resurrection and the Ascension together. Although Paul goes straight from Jesus being raised to his being seated at the right hand of God, it was his Ascension that got him there. Jesus' reigning now is more important in Paul's mind than his Ascension and enthronement, the events that started his reign.

While, in Romans, having all things under Jesus is something that awaits the end of the end times, in Ephesians Paul sees this as the situation now. There is no real contradiction here. If you are promised a job by someone utterly reliable you can be treated as already having the job in some ways, while you are still finishing off the tasks from your previous employment.

In the passage Paul makes the connection between Jesus reigning and the Church. Jesus is the head, the Church is his body, his fullness on earth. This is challenging and reassuring. We who are part of the Church are challenged to see ourselves for who we are, Jesus' body on earth, invigorated and directed by Jesus' Spirit, the Holy Spirit. For Paul, the language of being Jesus' body is not just a metaphor, but a reality. But this is also a comfort. We are not striving on Christ's behalf to change the world. Rather, by his Spirit Christ is striving with us and through us.

Colossians 3.1

> So if you have been raised with Christ, seek the things that are above, where Christ is, seated at the right hand of God.

The future breaks into the present again in Paul's thinking. Because we shall be raised with Christ, it has an impact on how we live now. We are the people who will be raised and so need to live as if we are that sort of people. To help us, Paul directs us to seek the things that are above, where Jesus is now. He is not just suggesting a spiritual meditation, but is reminding us that Jesus, who will raise us, is reigning now. So our actions on earth should be those that suit his people; our thoughts and actions are to be those of the servants of the king.

The Ascension in Paul's Letters

Philippians 3.14, 20–21

> I press on towards the goal for the prize of the heavenly call of God in Christ Jesus...
> But our citizenship is in heaven, and it is from there that we are expecting a Saviour, the Lord Jesus Christ. He will transform the body of our humiliation so that it may be conformed to the body of his glory, by the power that also enables him to make all things subject to himself.

Paul is used to the idea of citizenship. You may be living in one place, but your loyalty is to the place where you are a citizen. In these verses he is telling of his own inspiration in his faith. He is being called from heaven and to heaven. He is living in the light of his expectation of Jesus coming to save him from the body that will decay, and to give him a body of glory. This is a body fit for heaven, like the one the risen and ascended Christ has. This expectation shapes how he lives now, and how he wants his readers to live. His encouragement of his friends, in the light of these truths, is in verse 17: 'Brothers and sisters, join in imitating me and observe those who live according to the example you have in us.'

So, by his Ascension Jesus is in heaven, and he makes us, who are part of his Church, citizens of heaven too.

The final three verses are about Jesus being in heaven now. They imply the Ascension, since that is how Jesus got there. But each is more concerned with his current and future location than with his journey there.

Romans 10.6–7

> But the righteousness that comes from faith says, 'Do not say in your heart, "Who will ascend into heaven?" (that is, to bring Christ down) or "Who will descend into the abyss?"' (that is, to bring Christ up from the dead).

In this verse Paul simply assumes that Christ is in heaven, for how else could he be brought down?

1 Thessalonians 1.10

> ... and to wait for his Son from heaven, whom he raised from the dead – Jesus, who rescues us from the wrath that is coming.

In 1 Thessalonians this idea is repeated. Jesus will rescue us from the wrath of the final judgement when he comes. In the meantime, he is in heaven. This will make a difference to how we live now. For if we know we will be safe in the final judgement we can afford to take godly risks.

1 Thessalonians 4.16

> For the Lord himself, with a cry of command, with the archangel's call and with the sound of God's trumpet, will descend from heaven, and the dead in Christ will rise first.

By his Ascension Jesus is in heaven, from where he will come at the end of time to raise his followers from the dead.

A summary of Paul's thoughts on the Ascension

(a) Paul rarely refers to the Ascension as such. In all three places where he does, the pattern of ideas is of resurrection, Ascension and glorification or exaltation.
(b) Paul sees Jesus as being in heaven now, reigning with God the Father, at his right hand.
(c) While he is there Jesus is interceding for us, reconciling us to God.
(d) The Church is Jesus' body on earth; he is the Church's head in heaven. So Jesus' reign in heaven is intimately linked to our life on earth.
(e) When Jesus ascended he gave the gifts of the Holy Spirit. This Spirit is the spirit of Christ in his body on earth, the Church, which enables it to serve its heavenly head and king.

The Ascension in Paul's Letters

(f) Because our king is in heaven, that is where we belong. So although we live on earth, we are citizens of heaven and should behave as such.

(g) We know that we will be safe in the day of judgement because Jesus, who is in heaven, will come and save us. This too will affect how we live now.

Time and again Paul's thoughts turn to Jesus in heaven, to inspire us in our service of him on earth. His ideas are not just philosophical questionings but are the work of a pastor who is seeking to make a difference in and for the Church now.

5

The Ascension in 1 Peter, Revelation and Hebrews

The book of Hebrews can be regarded as a lengthy reflection on the Ascension and its implications for us. But before looking at it in detail, the other references to the Ascension in the Bible will be discussed.

1 Peter

> And baptism, which this prefigured, now saves you – not as a removal of dirt from the body, but as an appeal to God for a good conscience, through the resurrection of Jesus Christ, who has gone into heaven and is at the right hand of God, with angels, authorities, and powers made subject to him. (1 Peter 3.21–22)

Peter clearly speaks of the Ascension here, and links it to Jesus' being at the right hand of God, with all other powers under his authority. It seems likely that Peter saw Jesus' Ascension as the occasion when Jesus took up this authority, so the link is not just one of theology but also one of chronology, because one event, the Ascension, causes the other, Jesus reigning.

Revelation

Revelation is a letter written by John to the churches he cares for. In it he tells of a vision of Jesus, and in chapter 1 has this description:

Then I turned to see whose voice it was that spoke to me, and on turning I saw seven golden lampstands, and in the midst of the lampstands I saw one like the Son of Man, clothed with a long robe and with a golden sash across his chest. His head and his hair were white as white wool, white as snow; his eyes were like a flame of fire, his feet were like burnished bronze, refined as in a furnace, and his voice was like the sound of many waters. In his right hand he held seven stars, and from his mouth came a sharp, two-edged sword, and his face was like the sun shining with full force. (Revelation 1.12–16)

The description picks up the imagery of Daniel 7, but with a twist. For in Daniel 7.9 we read that in the prophet's vision:

… an Ancient One took his throne;
his clothing was white as snow,
    and the hair of his head like pure wool;
his throne was fiery flames,
    and its wheels were burning fire.

These characteristics of God on his throne are given to the 'one like the Son of Man' in Revelation 1. So the seer is making clear to his readers that he is seeing Jesus, ascended and with God, who having ascended is like God in every way, yet still a Son of Man.

This is the one who greets the churches with John and calls himself 'the ruler of the kings of the earth' (Revelation 1.5). In Revelation 3.21 we read: 'To the one who conquers I will give a place with me on my throne, just as I myself conquered and sat down with my Father on his throne.' For John, the Ascension is the triumph and enthronement of Jesus as Christ. Through his Ascension Jesus has come into heaven to receive the praise due for what he has done. As he stands in heaven, the Lamb who was slain is worshipped by all.

There are other allusions to the Ascension in the book of Revelation, but they tell us little more about it as a doctrine. For example, in Revelation 12.5–6 we read:

And she gave birth to a son, a male child, who is to rule all the nations with a rod of iron. But her child was snatched away and taken to God and to his throne; and the woman fled into the wilderness, where she has a place prepared by God, so that there she can be nourished for one thousand two hundred and sixty days.

Clearly this male child is Jesus since he is to rule the nations. The seer tells us he was taken to God and his throne and the woman fled to the wilderness. The woman at this point is the Church, who is being protected on earth by God.

Also, in Revelation 11 the two witnesses ascend to heaven in a cloud.

But these allusions add little to the vision of Chapter 5, where:

I looked, and I heard the voice of many angels surrounding the throne and the living creatures and the elders; they numbered myriads of myriads and thousands of thousands, singing with full voice,

> 'Worthy is the Lamb that was slaughtered
> to receive power and wealth and wisdom and might
> and honour and glory and blessing!'

Then I heard every creature in heaven and on earth and under the earth and in the sea, and all that is in them, singing,

> 'To the one seated on the throne and to the Lamb
> be blessing and honour and glory and might
> for ever and ever!'

(Revelation 5.11–13)

Hebrews

For the writer of the letter to Hebrews, Jesus' Ascension marks the end of his mission on earth and the beginning of the working out of its implications in heaven.

The Ascension in 1 Peter, Revelation and Hebrews

Where Luke shows the Ascension from the earthly viewpoint, the book of Hebrews takes up the story and looks at what happens in heaven. It does this not by imagining Jesus' journey once he was out of sight, but by looking at the theological implications of the Ascension.

Hebrews 1 tells of Jesus:

> He is the reflection of God's glory and the exact imprint of God's very being, and he sustains all things by his powerful word. When he had made purification for sins, he sat down at the right hand of the Majesty on high, having become as much superior to angels as the name he has inherited is more excellent than theirs.

The author then quotes several places in the Old Testament that speak of the coronation of God's chosen king (Psalm 2.7; 2 Samuel 7.14; 1 Chronicles 17.13; Psalm 45.6, 7; Psalm 110.1).

In Hebrews 2 the author applies Psalm 8 to Jesus. God made Jesus for a little while lower than the angels, as he became a human (Hebrews 2.9), but now he has crowned him with glory. Hebrews 2.10 makes it clear that the beginning of this crowning with glory came in Jesus' sufferings, in particular on the cross.

On the cross Jesus offered himself as a sacrifice once and for all; at his Ascension he took his human life thus offered totally to God and brought it to the throne of heaven. J. G. Davie puts it like this:

> By accomplishing this offering Christ made atonement, and this act is a process: the dying, by which His blood is outpoured (2.14; 9.15); the rising, by which 'God brings again from the dead the great shepherd of the sheep with the blood of the eternal covenant' (13.20), and the ascending, by which He enters into heaven itself with the blood (9.12, 14, 25; 10.19) 'now to appear before the face of God for us' (9.24). (1958, p. 66)

Hebrews 4 tells us that when he came into heaven at his Ascension Jesus was made High Priest.

> Since, then, we have a great high priest who has passed through the heavens, Jesus, the Son of God, let us hold fast to our confession. For we do not have a high priest who is unable to sympathize with our weaknesses, but we have one who in every respect has been tested as we are, yet without sin. Let us therefore approach the throne of grace with boldness, so that we may receive mercy and find grace to help in time of need. (Hebrews 4.14–16)

There he offers, not just his death, but his whole human life. This isn't just a payment of a debt we incur, but the ongoing, living reconciliations between people and God seen in Jesus' presence at God's right hand.

In chapter 5 we hear more about this priesthood.

> ... having been made perfect, he became the source of eternal salvation for all who obey him, having been designated by God a high priest according to the order of Melchizedek. (Hebrews 5.9–10)

Jesus' priesthood is of an older order than that of Aaron. It is like that of Melchizedek the king and priest of Salem, to whom Abraham offered a tenth of his spoil after defeating the kings in Genesis 14 (Hebrews 7.1–3). This picks up the ideas of Hebrews 1, that Jesus is the king who reigns with God, through being the priest who offers his life to God, on behalf of humanity.

Jesus' offering of himself is not just about God but about us, so in chapter 9 we read:

> ... how much more will the blood of Christ, who through the eternal Spirit offered himself without blemish to God, purify our conscience from dead works to worship the living God! (Hebrews 9.14)

Jesus' blood is offered to God, as his life, and acts to set us free from our fear of judgement, so that we may truly worship God with our lives.

> For Christ did not enter a sanctuary made by human hands, a mere copy of the true one, but he entered into heaven itself, now to appear in the presence of God on our behalf. (Hebrews 9.24)

This is why Jesus' humanity is vital. He is appearing as a human high priest before God, so that in him God and humanity are reconciled. This reconciliation will be eternal:

> But when Christ had offered for all time a single sacrifice for sins, 'he sat down at the right hand of God', and since then has been waiting 'until his enemies would be made a footstool for his feet'. (Hebrews 10.12–13)

Knowing he is there for us, reconciling us to God, we,

> have confidence to enter the sanctuary by the blood of Jesus, by the new and living way that he opened for us through the curtain (that is, through his flesh), and since we have a great priest over the house of God, let us approach with a true heart in full assurance of faith, with our hearts sprinkled clean from an evil conscience and our bodies washed with pure water. Let us hold fast to the confession of our hope without wavering, for he who has promised is faithful. And let us consider how to provoke one another to love and good deeds, not neglecting to meet together, as is the habit of some, but encouraging one another, and all the more as you see the Day approaching. (Hebrews 10.19–25)

So, Jesus' presence in heaven opens up a way for us to come into God's presence. He gives us confidence to claim his reconciliation for each of us, by prayer, and inspires us to live the way he calls us to. This reflection on the reality in heaven is not about giving us pious thoughts, but about motivating the Church to goodness as it struggles and suffers in this world. This inspiration comes not only from Jesus, but from all who have lived his way by faith (Hebrews 11).

The Missing Ending

As well as by prayer, we receive the benefits of Christ's priestly acts in communion, since '[w]e have an altar from which those who officiate in the tent have no right to eat' (Hebrews 13.10). This enables us to offer our sacrifice with his:

> Through him, then, let us continually offer a sacrifice of praise to God, that is, the fruit of lips that confess his name. Do not neglect to do good and to share what you have, for such sacrifices are pleasing to God. (Hebrews 13.15–16)

To summarize, Hebrews is an extended reflection on Jesus' priesthood in heaven, which started at his Ascension. He is both priest and king. As king he reigns with God over the universe – a human is on the throne with God. As priest he is for ever offering his life lived in obedience to God, lived obeying God even into and through death. Thus, he offers a totally perfect human life to God, on our behalf, so that we with our imperfect lives can be reconciled to God.

His presence in heaven opens up the way for us to go there; he is the pioneer for humanity. His priesthood also enables us to come before God in prayer, and to share in his sacrifice in Holy Communion. Together with the faith of those who have been God's servants before us, these inspire us in our lives to praise God and to do good.

6

So, What did Happen?

The Ascension on Easter Day

From our review of Luke, John and Matthew, it is clear that the Gospels are unanimous. Jesus went to his Father and was exalted – he received his glory – on the same day as he rose. However, they are also clear that it is a separate event from the resurrection. So, Jesus says to Mary in the garden, 'Do not hold on to me, because I have not yet ascended to the Father. But go to my brothers and say to them, "I am ascending to my Father and your Father, to my God and your God"' (John 20.17). When he sees his disciples later, he comes from beyond the world, and breathes the Holy Spirit on them. This is a sign that he has ascended to the Father, since in John 16 Jesus says, '[I]t is to your advantage that I go away, for if I do not go away, the Advocate will not come to you; but if I go, I will send him to you' (John 16.7).

So, Jesus was resurrected, met with Mary and then ascended and was exalted. In Luke it is less clear that there is a separation between the resurrection and the exaltation. On the road to Emmaus Jesus says to the two, 'Was it not necessary that the Messiah should suffer these things and then enter into his glory?' (Luke 24.26), which implies that Jesus has already ascended and been exalted. However, at the end of the chapter we read that on Easter Day, very late, he and his disciples go out to Bethany and Jesus blesses his disciples and parts from them to heaven.

In Matthew, when Jesus meets with his disciples on a mountain, Jesus tells them: 'All authority in heaven and on earth has been given to me' (Matthew 28.18). This recalls the passage in Daniel 7, where the prophet sees

The Missing Ending

... one like a human being
   coming with the clouds of heaven.
And he came to the Ancient One
   and was presented before him.
To him was given dominion
   and glory and kingship,
that all peoples, nations, and languages
   should serve him.
(Daniel 7.13–14)

Since Jesus, who regularly calls himself the Son of Man, is now saying that he has been given all authority, it implies that he has already come to the Ancient One and been given his authority. So, before his final appearance to his disciples, he has already ascended to his Father and been exalted.

What is clear is that we need to distinguish the Ascension as exaltation from the Ascension as farewell.

The Ascension as exaltation is unseen, unwitnessed, as mysterious as the resurrection. However, just as with the resurrection its *results* can be seen. The resurrection gave Jesus a new body, one that would not die, fit for heaven. The Ascension, as exaltation, gave him a new place to be, from where he came to the disciples to show them that he is alive. If this is true, then the resurrection appearances are as much exaltation appearances. And the curious question of where Jesus is when he is not with the disciples is resolved – he is beyond this world in heaven. That is why doors are no problem, since Jesus is coming from outside the physical universe.

What Luke describes in Luke 24.50–53 is the last of Jesus' appearances to his disciples. It is a farewell appearance, where he blesses them as the High Priest. The blessing in a service is the point at which we are drawn again into the presence of God for the purpose of being sent out, *with* the presence of God, to serve him in the world. So the disciples respond with worship, and prayer in the Temple, to ready themselves for service. The joy they experience on this occasion would be odd if they saw it as a final farewell to Jesus as such. Rather, it is a farewell to *see-*

ing Jesus, but not to *knowing* Jesus. In the passage in Matthew 28, Matthew makes this clear:

> Now the eleven disciples went to Galilee, to the mountain to which Jesus had directed them. When they saw him, they worshipped him; but some doubted. And Jesus came and said to them, 'All authority in heaven and on earth has been given to me. Go therefore and make disciples of all nations, baptizing them in the name of the Father and of the Son and of the Holy Spirit, and teaching them to obey everything that I have commanded you. And remember, I am with you always, to the end of the age.' (Matthew 28.16–20)

Matthew does not need to record Jesus' physical farewell, since the important thing is that Jesus will be with his disciples, inspiring and directing their service.

The Ascension 40 days later

When Luke wrote Acts, his first scene was what we call the Ascension. From his Gospel, it is clear that Luke thought that the Ascension of Jesus to his Father happened on Easter Day. However, Luke tells of Jesus' last physical appearance to his disciples in such a way as to emphasize his exaltation. This does not mean that he necessarily saw this as the first occasion of his exaltation; rather, he tells of the final appearance in such a way that the disciples know it will be final and are assured of Jesus' true status as Lord.

By starting with the Ascension Luke recalls his ending to his Gospel. These two accounts of Jesus' final appearance to his disciples are the pivot on which Luke's double work turns. We can see this from the way in which Luke points towards the Ascension in his Gospel, in his telling of the Transfiguration, and his note at Luke 9.51, 'When the days drew near for him to be taken up, he set his face to go to Jerusalem.' This pivot turns the story from the acts of Jesus in the flesh, to the acts of

The Missing Ending

the exalted, ascended Lord Jesus Christ, by the Spirit through his witnesses. It is the first scene of a book that will tell of how the apostles did indeed go to Jerusalem, Judea, Samaria and as far as Rome.

As we look at the passage in more detail it is important to see what this narrative is not about. What it's not about is a naive belief in a triple-decker universe, with heaven somewhere up there above the clouds. Rowan Williams wrote,

> 'He ascended into heaven' say the creeds, recalling the stories in Luke's Gospel and the Acts of the Apostles about how Jesus says goodbye to the disciples and is carried into heaven. This is pictorial language of course, not to be interpreted as if the Bible were thinking of a sort of space travel. The biblical writers knew quite well that God did not live in a literal place above the clouds, but they happily used the strong images of the Old Testament poems and psalms to tell us that after a while Jesus appeared no more in a material form to his disciples. (Williams, 2007, p. 93)

As we look at the passage it is worth having in mind the imagery of Elijah's assumption, of God appearing in a cloud to Moses on Sinai, of the glory of God appearing in the Temple.

> So when they had come together, they asked him, 'Lord, is this the time when you will restore the kingdom to Israel?' He replied, 'It is not for you to know the times or periods that the Father has set by his own authority. But you will receive power when the Holy Spirit has come upon you; and you will be my witnesses in Jerusalem, in all Judea and Samaria, and to the ends of the earth.' When he had said this, as they were watching, he was lifted up, and a cloud took him out of their sight. While he was going and they were gazing up towards heaven, suddenly two men in white robes stood by them. They said, 'Men of Galilee, why do you stand looking up towards heaven? This Jesus, who has been taken up from you into heaven, will come in the same way as you saw him go into heaven.'

So, What did Happen?

Then they returned to Jerusalem from the mount called Olivet, which is near Jerusalem, a sabbath day's journey away.' (Acts 1.6–12)

It is important to see the verse that describes Jesus' departure in its context in Acts. Luke introduces it by describing a conversation between Jesus and his disciples about Israel. In their question to Jesus the disciples showed what they were expecting. Now that he had been raised and exalted to God, surely now God would fulfil the promises to Israel.

They were still expecting the kingdom that God would bring to be a re-establishment of Israel as an autonomous country ruled by a Davidic king, the Messiah. This surely would be the outcome of the Messiah having come, this was what the reign of the Messiah was about, was it not? The physical land of Israel was still filled with meaning for them, despite the experiences of the exile, when the Jews had discovered how to sing the songs of God in a foreign land.

Jesus has a three-fold answer. First, he tells them that the times are set by the Father's authority and they have to live with that. He is saying neither 'yes' nor 'no' but is refusing to give a time-bound answer. For God is about to restore the kingdom, but not in a way they will recognize and not in a time frame they can comprehend. With the resurrection and the Ascension God has acted decisively, in an ultimate way in the world. They mark the beginning of the end of the world. But we live in the in-between times: the beginning of the end has come, but not yet the end of the end. The fact that this in-between time has lasted 2,000 years already is bemusing to us as humans but, as the psalmist says, 'a thousand years in your sight are like yesterday when it is past, or like a watch in the night' (Psalm 90.4). So Jesus tells them not to be concerned with time; it is not the important aspect of what God is doing.

Next Jesus points them to a new geography. Up to now they have been focused on Israel as the place that God is interested in, where God will be glorified. But now 'you will be my witnesses in Jerusalem, in all Judea and Samaria, and to the ends of the earth' (Acts 1.8). They will return to Jerusalem, and it is there that they will receive the Holy Spirit, there that they will know God's presence and power, fulfilling all that God looked for from Israel. But the aim of this is not to stay in Jerusalem, but to go to Judea, to the despised Samaritans – thus breaking the ethnic and religious divides that were around Israel – and to the ends of the earth. They are no longer to look for the end *time* for God's ultimate action, but for the end *places* where they will go for him and see what he will do there.

The third answer Jesus gives to the question is in dramatic action that follows. Having 'presented himself alive to them by many convincing proofs, appearing to them over the course of forty days and speaking about the kingdom of God' (Acts 1.3), Jesus acts so that they do not see him physically any more. But that does not mean he is not active any more, as the rest of the book will show.

An acted answer

> ... as they were watching, he was lifted up, and a cloud took him out of their sight. (Acts 1.9)

> Our Lord accommodated his actions to his expressions, and symbolised both his triumph and his destination by parting from his disciples and this world of ours in a manner so vividly described in the Acts of the Apostles. Acted parable is a common feature of biblical prophecy. (Thompson, 1964, p. 13)

Where did it happen?

If it is right to see this action as part of the answer, then nothing about what happens will be in the narrative by chance. That includes the location. We have to wait until verse 12 to find out where Jesus and his disciples are, since there we read, 'Then they returned to Jerusalem from the mount called Olivet.'

The Mount of Olives plays an important role in the Gospels. It is from the Mount of Olives that Jesus comes into Jerusalem on

So, What did Happen?

Palm Sunday, to lead a demonstration and confront the authorities. The Mount of Olives is the place where Jesus stands as he prophesies doom for Jerusalem, recalling Zechariah's vision of the Lord God coming to the Mount of Olives (Zechariah 1.1–5). It is to the Mount of Olives that Jesus regularly goes to pray. The Garden of Gethsemane is on the Mount of Olives and is the scene of Jesus' great prayer on the night he is betrayed.

We should not overlook that this is a mountain, and the importance of mountains in the Bible. Abraham is asked to offer his son on Mount Moriah, the law is given to Moses on Sinai, Elijah faces the prophets of Baal on Mount Carmel and then flees to Mount Horeb. The mount in Jerusalem is known as Mount Zion, and Isaiah looks to the day when the Lord's Temple is established as the highest of the mountains.

In the Bible mountains are places where people meet with God. It may be in private prayer or in an individual revelation of God, as for Elijah and Moses, or a great sense of God's presence as on Sinai. So the fact that they are on a mountain is not surprising; it is the sort of place where you experience God. This signals that what Jesus did was not merely to say his last physical goodbye but to point to the presence of God.

Finally, the Mount of Olives is near Jerusalem, but it's *not* Jerusalem. By going here, Jesus is beginning the disciples' journey outwards from Jerusalem. He could have ascended from the Temple mount, but instead he goes out of Jerusalem, to the place where he pronounced judgement on Jerusalem. This is the beginning of a new way of seeing Jerusalem, where it is the scene of God's action in Jesus but is no longer the centre of worship of God in the world. That is about to be transferred with Jesus' Ascension to a place beyond the world, where Jesus is at God's right hand. In John, Jesus makes it clear that he sees his body as the new temple (John 2.19), the place where humanity comes to meet with God. In the Ascension this place is taken by Jesus into heaven, so the place where humanity meets with God is now in Jesus' humanity as he offers it to the Father in heaven. This means that no place on earth can be seen as the Temple where God meets with humans, and so we must worship in spirit and in truth (John 4.21–24).

How did he go?

Luke tells how Jesus went in three ways:

Visibly

The disciples saw Jesus go. This in a sense was different from other times when Jesus left them after his post-resurrection appearances. In Luke 24.31 Jesus just vanished when his disciples finally recognized him over a meal in Emmaus. But on this occasion, his followers saw him go. This lets them know that the phase of the appearances is over. It also emphasizes that Jesus has bodily gone to heaven. He is still fully human, and you can't be fully human without a body.

Lifted up

The word used in Acts is *epairo*, which means 'to raise up', so Jesus is not the one who does the action but is lifted by someone else in the Acts narrative. Where the Bible uses a verb in the passive voice the implication is that God is the one who is doing the action. This is quite common in the Bible – it is a way of speaking of God's activity without naming God, something that was avoided, to keep the name of God holy.

So, in Acts Jesus is taken up to heaven. It could be that this is just what it looked like to the disciples, as Gerrit Scott Dawson says: 'He did not flap his arms and fly under evident human power. He was taken up in the sky until the cloud hid him from their sight' (Dawson, 2004, p. 38). Or it could be that the Ascension is primarily an act of God, Father, Son and Holy Spirit. So, as for Jesus' humanity, he was taken up, but his divinity was involved in the action. This is important since elsewhere the Bible speaks of Jesus actively going up (*anabaino*) to heaven (John 3.13; 6.62).

But why did Jesus go *up*? He could have gone sideways or down, why go up? This feature is what makes some doubt the truth of this story, for it seems to imply that Jesus and his followers believed in a heaven above the clouds, something we

So, What did Happen?

cannot accept today. But if we see this as an acted parable it makes sense that Jesus goes *up* to symbolize going out of this universe to where God is, to heaven. A disappearance into the ground would have a different symbolism entirely. Despite the fact that we know that God is not above the clouds we still look *up* when we are thinking of God. It is part of our stereotypical and symbolical language. F. F. Bruce in his *Commentary on the Book of Acts* says, 'Anyone appearing to leave the earth's surface must appear to spectators to be ascending and so when the cloud enveloped the visible form of the Lord, His disciples stood looking steadfastly in Heaven as he went' (1954, p. 40).

We affirm with Calvin: 'What? Do we place Christ midway among the spheres? Or do we build a cottage for him among the planets? Heaven we regard as the magnificent palace of God, far outstripping all this world's fabric' (Beveridge and Bonnet, eds, 1998, p. 270). But we still look up as the direction of what is beyond us as humans. We look towards the stars and out into space, away from our tiny globe of blue and green, when we look towards what is beyond us.

A cloud took him out of their sight

Since this is an action with meaning – an acted metaphor, if you like – we should not see this simply as the sort of cloud that you see on mountains. The glory of God was represented as a cloud many times in the Old Testament (for example, Exodus 19.9; 40.34; 2 Chronicles 5.14). One nuance here is that the most straightforward translation of the Greek would be 'a cloud came under to lift him up from them from their sight.' This makes it clear not just that the cloud hid him, but that the cloud itself was the thing that carried Jesus off. So, as the disciples watch, the cloud which is the presence of God takes Jesus out of their sight. They know that Jesus has gone to his Father; they have seen his Father's glory come to embrace Jesus and carry him home.

Knowing Daniel 7 it would be easy for them to see this as a sign that the Jesus whom they can no longer see is now 'coming with the clouds of heaven' to the Ancient of Days, his Father, to receive his authority and dominion.

When preaching on the Ascension in the fifth century, John Chrysostom compared Elijah's assumption to Jesus' Ascension:

> For when it was necessary for the servant to be called, a chariot was sent, but when the Son, a royal throne, and not simply a royal throne but the Father's. For concerning the Father Isaiah says: 'Behold, the Lord sitteth upon a light cloud.' Since the Father sits upon a cloud, He sends the cloud for the Son. (Chrysostom, *Homily on the Ascension of our Lord*)

Where did he go?

Luke is very quiet on what happened next to Jesus. Second-century writers of apocryphal gospels and apocalypses were less reticent and were willing to tell great tales of Jesus ascending through the heavens, being worshipped by the angels. But for Luke what needed to be said about Jesus' Ascension had been said in the image of the cloud of God's glory carrying him away. What happened for Jesus after that was not Luke's focus. His viewpoint remained with the disciples. However, to show the disciples where Jesus had gone they are granted the presence of two men in white, who say to them, 'Men of Galilee, why do you stand looking up towards heaven? This Jesus, who has been taken up from you into heaven, will come in the same way as you saw him go into heaven' (Acts 1.11). So they know he has gone to heaven, and that some time he will return. This completes Jesus' answer to them. God is bringing in his kingdom, but it is not by restoring Israel to self-governance. Rather, it is by Jesus going to heaven to the Father's right hand and sending them the Holy Spirit to enable them to witness to him to the ends of the earth. The time aspect is still in God's hands and Jesus will return physically in God's time; meantime they are to focus instead on place.

So, there was a secret Ascension on Easter Day where Jesus was exalted, and a symbolic one on the fortieth day, so that

So, What did Happen?

Jesus' followers would know that he had been exalted. Although Luke knew that the exaltation had already occurred, he records indications of Jesus' exaltation in this narrative to show that it is not just a farewell. It is the beginning of Christ's being active as king, by his spirit through his witnesses.

7

Why in Heaven did it Happen?

Jesus' Ascension made a difference on earth and in heaven. First, we will look at what the Bible says about the meaning of the Ascension from the heavenly point of view. This in turn will help us to see the implications for us on earth.

Made both Lord and Christ

After the description of the Ascension in Acts it is referred to several times in the preaching and witness of the disciples. In Acts 2, on the Day of Pentecost Peter preaches to the crowd who are attracted by the outpouring of words from the disciples, and says:

> This Jesus God raised up, and of that all of us are witnesses. Being therefore exalted at the right hand of God, and having received from the Father the promise of the Holy Spirit, he has poured out this that you both see and hear. For David did not ascend into the heavens, but he himself says,
> 'The Lord said to my Lord,
> "Sit at my right hand,
>   until I make your enemies your footstool."'
> Therefore let the entire house of Israel know with certainty that God has made him both Lord and Messiah, this Jesus whom you crucified.
> (Acts 2.32–36)

So, Luke summarizes Peter's message by saying that the people of Jerusalem had Jesus killed, but God raised him from death and, through the Ascension to heaven, Jesus was exalted. This involves sitting at God's right hand and being named as both Lord and Christ.

Similarly, in Acts 3 the summary of Peter's sermon includes:

> In this way God fulfilled what he had foretold through all the prophets, that his Messiah would suffer. Repent therefore, and turn to God so that your sins may be wiped out, so that times of refreshing may come from the presence of the Lord, and that he may send the Messiah appointed for you, that is, Jesus, who must remain in heaven until the time of universal restoration that God announced long ago through his holy prophets. (Acts 3.18–21)

When Stephen is preaching to those who are accusing him of blasphemy he has a vision of Jesus:

> But filled with the Holy Spirit, he gazed into heaven and saw the glory of God and Jesus standing at the right hand of God. 'Look,' he said, 'I see the heavens opened and the Son of Man standing at the right hand of God!' (Acts 7.55–56)

For Luke, it is clear that Jesus' Ascension is not just about Jesus leaving the world, but about him coming to God and being given the authority of Lord, and the role of Messiah.

This is supported by Paul's letters. In Philippians 2 we read,

> Therefore God also highly exalted him
>   and gave him the name
>   that is above every name,
> so that at the name of Jesus
>   every knee should bend,
>   in heaven and on earth and under the earth,
> and every tongue should confess
>   that Jesus Christ is Lord,
>   to the glory of God the Father.
> (Philippians 2.9–11)

The Missing Ending

For both Luke and Paul the heart of the Christian message is that people know that Jesus is *Lord*, that he has been given dominion over all things, and that they need to respond to this. For example, Paul in Romans 10.9 says, 'If you confess with your lips that Jesus is Lord and believe in your heart that God raised him from the dead, you will be saved.' This title of Lord, and indeed of Messiah or Christ, has become so familiar that it has lost its impact on us.

Although 'Lord' could be used of one human by another in the Bible, it is most clearly used by God's people of their supreme Lord, God himself. Indeed, calling God 'Lord' was second nature to Jews. To avoid the use of God's name, and so any chance to taking God's name in vain, they used the term 'Lord' of God. Even where the Hebrew Scriptures have the consonants 'YHWH', the Jews read instead the Hebrew word *adonai*, which means 'Lord'. (To help them remember this, when the vowels were added to the Hebrew text in the eighth or ninth century AD, the vowels of 'adonai' were put over the consonants of 'yhwh'. When translated by some scholars who were unaware of this the name of God was translated as 'yehowah', that is, Jehovah. This is not the name of God, but a name that comes from fallible translators.) So calling Jesus 'Lord', in this context, is to give him the title of God, the name that is indeed over every other name.

But in Acts Peter is recorded as saying that God has made Jesus 'Messiah' (or 'Christ', the Greek version of the Hebrew word 'Messiah', both meaning 'anointed one'). We tend to think of Jesus being Messiah through his earthly life, but it may be that the reason Jesus disowns the title so often in the Gospels is that he sees himself as becoming the Messiah, but not yet the Messiah. It is only through his death, resurrection and Ascension that he is appointed Messiah by God. Only through his obedience to what God has called him to does he come into this title. Now he reigns as God's anointed and appointed one, in heaven, and one day will come as Messiah from heaven.

So, by his Ascension Jesus is exalted, he is to be known as 'Lord' just as God is, and as 'Messiah' the human who acts on God's behalf. He sits at God's right hand, now, reigning with God the Father now. His reign may not be fully clear on earth but he reigns in heaven, '... until he has put all his enemies under his feet. The last enemy to be destroyed is death' (1 Corinthians 15.25–26).

Glorified

Associated with this idea of Jesus being Lord and Christ is the idea that he has been glorified by his Ascension. Paul tells his listeners in Colossians 3.1–4 that they will be glorified with Christ if they seek the things above:

> So if you have been raised with Christ, seek the things that are above, where Christ is, seated at the right hand of God. Set your minds on things that are above, not on things that are on earth, for you have died, and your life is hidden with Christ in God. When Christ who is your life is revealed, then you also will be revealed with him in glory.

But what is glorification? Well, glory is the beauty and brightness of the presence of God, so for a human to be glorified is for them to be so totally open to the presence of God that God's brightness shines through. Although Jesus was always God's Son, God as a human being, when he ascended to heaven his humanity was brought fully into the presence of God the Father, and God's beauty and honour is to be found completely reflected in Jesus' human nature in heaven. Our hope is that our human nature will similarly reflect God, not just fully in heaven one day, but each day on earth while we wait.

Another way of looking at this is to be found in the idea of 'Christus Victor' or Christ as Victor. The Ascension is one part of the process by which Jesus achieved victory over evil. His death, his descent into hell, his resurrection and his Ascension together brought us deliverance from darkness into light. As J. G. Davies explains in his book on the Ascension:

By the cross he triumphed over the principalities and powers; by his *descensus* He has entered the abyss which is the very abode of Satan, and by his exaltation, through Resurrection and Ascension, He has become the 'head of all principality and power', the One to whom all created things, in heaven and on earth, are subject. (1958, pp. 62–3)

Paul uses the idea of Jesus' victory parade to explain why Jesus gave the gifts of the Holy Spirit:

But each of us was given grace according to the measure of Christ's gift. Therefore it is said,
'When he ascended on high he made captivity itself a captive;
   he gave gifts to his people.'
(When it says, 'He ascended', what does it mean but that he had also descended into the lower parts of the earth? He who descended is the same one who ascended far above all the heavens, so that he might fill all things.)
(Ephesians 4.7–10)

Interestingly, in Psalm 68, which Paul is quoting, the image is of God going up in victory *taking* gifts from those he has conquered. But for Paul Jesus' victory is so great that he *gives* gifts to people, those whom he is liberating through his victory.

A human at God's right hand

Another aspect of the Ascension which we see in Acts is that Jesus who is ascended is a human who is at God's right hand. It is not just as God that Jesus has ascended but as the God-human who was born a human, and is for ever a human. So, in Acts 17.31 we hear of Paul saying, '[God] has fixed a day on which he will have the world judged in righteousness by a man whom he has appointed, and of this he has given assurance to all by raising him from the dead.' Peter tells us,

Why in Heaven did it Happen?

> And baptism, which this prefigured, now saves you – not as a removal of dirt from the body, but as an appeal to God for a good conscience, through the resurrection of Jesus Christ, who has gone into heaven and is at the right hand of God, with angels, authorities, and powers made subject to him. (1 Peter 3.21–22)

It is the same Jesus who was raised who has gone into heaven. Luke in his narrative has underlined that Jesus went bodily into heaven, and so it is a human at God's right hand. Here there are three important things.

First, Jesus is still human with a human body. This means that the one whom God has appointed to judge humans is not someone who used to be human, but someone who is still human.

Second, he is in the presence of God. A human is at God's right hand. This is the pledge that we as humans can one day also be in God's direct presence. This has been a source of wonder for Christians down the centuries. Irenaeus wrote of 'the word of God, our Lord Jesus Christ, who did, through his transcendent love, become what we are, that He might bring us to be even what he is himself' (*Against the Heresies* 5).

This idea was taken up by early Christians in the idea of Jesus as the first fruits of humanity. So, for example, John Chrysostom said in his Homily on the Ascension of our Lord, '[A]nd today is the foundation of these benefits [i.e., our reconciliation with God], for as he assumed the first fruits of our nature, so He took them up to the Lord.' He continues:

> For as it happens in a field full of corn, when a man takes a few ears of corn and makes a small sheaf and offers it to God, he blesses the whole cornfield by means of this sheaf, so Christ has done this also, and through that one flesh and first fruits has made our race to be blessed.

The Ascension brings into being the full reconciliation between humanity and God, since God put himself in our place when Jesus was made human at the incarnation, and humanity was brought to God's place in the Ascension. In the resurrection, where death was conquered, Christ's humanity was transformed so as not be mortal; in the Ascension that transformed humanity entered a new way of existing in heaven. In heaven Jesus' humanity enters the Temple of God, heaven itself, and is offered as the first fruits of humanity, making all humanity holy. He is the ascended Head of the Church, and '[h]is Body glorified through Resurrection and Ascension, is now the centre and substance of His mystical Body, the Church – hence the virtual identity between them. But since "it is not yet made manifest what we shall be" [1 John 3.2], since, that is to say, our present condition is in contrast with His present condition, the two must be distinguished in our understanding. We have received the pledge but not the fullness of our inheritance' (Davies, 1958, p. 173).

Finally, Jesus is at the right hand of God. But where is that? Is it a place or a metaphor for sharing God's authority and power? The Bible gives mixed messages on this. In Acts 7.55–56 Stephen sees heaven opened and Jesus at God's right hand, which implies that somewhere there is a place where Jesus is. The early Fathers such as Irenaeus and Tertullian, in rejecting those (known as the docetists) who said Jesus only seemed to be human but wasn't really, emphasize that Jesus ascended bodily. This fits with what it means to be human: it includes having a body, and if we have a body it has to be in a *place*. Otherwise, we are disembodied and so not fully human any more, but rather a spirit who was human once.

But in the last chapter we saw that 'heaven' is not to be found in this universe. And the phrase 'the right hand of God' has a meaning that is beyond a physical location. It is about sharing in God's power and authority. It is better to see 'place' in this context as more about relationship than space as such. So, Jesus as God came to humanity's 'place', so that Jesus as a human could go to God's 'place'.

Why in Heaven did it Happen?

To fill everything in every way

Ephesians 4.9–10 is the only passage about the Ascension which directly says why it happened. In Ephesians 4.10 Christ ascended 'that he might fill all things'. Christ filling the universe with his divine activity claims it as his rightful possession – he is its governor, its ruler.

This filling everything led to some seeing Christ's Ascension as into being everywhere. Luther for example, in defending the real presence of Jesus in the bread and wine of communion, argued that Jesus' Ascension was into being everywhere: since he is divine he cannot be confined to one place. If we think that heaven is wherever Jesus is active, it can't be a localized place at all.

This is countered by those, such as Karl Barth, who affirm that Jesus' *body* when ascended is in one place, but he is also God and so as God can be everywhere. What links us on earth to Jesus our Head in heaven is the Holy Spirit.

The High Priest in heaven's temple

So, Jesus has ascended, and is a human in heaven, but what is he doing there? We have seen that he is the Messiah, the anointed one, and that this works out in his reigning in heaven, at God's right hand. But the Israelites were not only looking for a Messianic king. In Jewish thinking there were three roles that people were anointed for: king, priest and prophet. (As king see 1 Samuel 10.1; 16.13; 2 Samuel 2.1; Psalms 18.50; 20.6. As priest see, e.g., Exodus 2.7; 30.30; 40.13, 15; Leviticus 4. For prophet see Psalm 105.15; Isaiah 61.1: usually the prophet's way was more that of having the Spirit of God on them, rather than being physically anointed by another human, but they were still thought of as anointed, since the physical anointing was a symbol of God's picking someone out to serve him.)

The book of Hebrews is an extended discourse on how Jesus is the High Priest and King of Israel, who has entered into heaven. This journey started with Jesus' life on earth and particularly with his death on the cross, where he gave his life (not just his death) to become an atoning sacrifice for all. But if we look at the Jewish sacrificial system we see that it has two stages.

In Exodus 30 and Leviticus 16 the procedure for the sin offering is described. In Exodus 16 the incense altar, which is to be in front of the Ark of the Covenant in the Most Holy Place, is described. The altar will be the place where incense is burned each day. Once a year a ritual is performed to ensure that it remains holy (Exodus 30.10). A bull is slaughtered *outside* the Tent of Meeting, and then its blood, which represents its life, is taken into the Most Holy Place, and sprinkled on the incense altar. Similarly in Leviticus 16, the sin offering is described. After preparatory sacrifices to cleanse the priests and the Tent of Meeting, a goat and a bull are slaughtered at the entrance to the tent, but that is not the sacrifice in itself. Their blood is then brought in and sprinkled on the front of the mercy seat, which is the cover over the Ark of the Covenant.

So the death of the animal is not enough: it must then have its blood, the symbol of its life, offered in the Most Holy Place.

Just so, the book of Hebrews says of Jesus, 'When he had made purification for sins, he sat down at the right hand of the Majesty on high' (Hebrews 1.3).

How did Jesus offer this sacrifice?

> But when Christ came as a high priest of the good things that have come, then through the greater and perfect tent (not made with hands, that is, not of this creation), he entered once for all into the Holy Place, not with the blood of goats and calves, but with his own blood, thus obtaining eternal redemption. (Hebrews 9.11–12)

Jesus' death was the equivalent of the bull being slaughtered, and his entry into heaven was the equivalent of the sacrifice being offered by the blood, the symbol not just of his death but also of his life, being brought into the Most Holy Place.

Jesus is the High Priest in heaven offering his whole life as a sacrifice to God. He is also the mediator of the new covenant

(Hebrews 9.15). To be a mediator is to be the person who brings parties together, enabling them to relate to each other. Because of this, 'we have confidence to enter the sanctuary by the blood of Jesus, by the new and living way that he opened for us through the curtain (that is, through his flesh)' (Hebrews 10.19–20).

Christ intercedes for us, since, as the author says, 'he holds his priesthood permanently, because he continues for ever. Consequently he is able for all time to save those who approach God through him, since he always lives to make intercession for them' (Hebrews 7.24–25). This is not begging a God who does not want to know about us. Rather, it is God the Son, as a human, offering himself, all he is, to God the Father on our behalf, and bringing all that we need as his family on earth into the heart of the Godhead. In himself Jesus brings humanity before God. His humanity is a life lived totally in relationship with God the Father, in total obedience. He has shown complete love of God and of others all the way to and in his death. This he brings into God's presence: this *is* the intercession, a perfect humanity before God. Jesus in heaven is the Head of his body on earth, so by holding his humanity within the Godhead, his Church is held there too.

To prepare a place for you

As well as interceding for us, Jesus' presence as human is a pledge that we will join with him in our time. Jesus promised this to his disciples when he was with them on the night before he died. In John 14 he says, 'In my Father's house there are many dwelling-places. If it were not so, would I have told you that I go to prepare a place for you? And if I go and prepare a place for you, I will come again and will take you to myself, so that where I am, there you may be also' (John 14.2–3)

This is the promise that makes us citizens of heaven.

Giving gifts to humans – sending the Holy Spirit

Jesus said in John 16, 'Nevertheless, I tell you the truth: it is to your advantage that I go away, for if I do not go away, the Advocate will not come to you; but if I go, I will send him to you' (John 16.7).

On the Day of Pentecost Peter explained to those who gathered, 'Being therefore exalted at the right hand of God, and having received from the Father the promise of the Holy Spirit, he has poured out this that you both see and hear' (Acts 2.33). The coming of the Holy Spirit to earth is the confirmation that Jesus is ascended, exalted and glorified. The Spirit enables Jesus' body on earth, the Church, to be his witnesses, to the ends of the earth.

8

Why on Earth did it Happen?

What difference does this make to us? We have seen the difference that Jesus bringing his humanity into heaven and being exalted there makes in heaven, but what are the implication on earth?

Affirmation of the resurrection

As part of the 'movement of salvation', the Ascension plays its part in affirming all that has gone before. The movement of salvation is what is described in the Apostles' Creed where we say of Jesus that he was:

> born of the Virgin Mary,
> suffered under Pontius Pilate,
> was crucified, died, and was buried;
> he descended to the dead.
> On the third day he rose again;
> he ascended into heaven,
> he is seated at the right hand of the Father.

The 'movement of salvation' is what we read about in Philippians 2 – Jesus descends from his place of equality with God, taking the form of a human servant, in the incarnation. He lives a human life of total obedience and humbles himself even to the point of dying on the cross. Then in 1 Peter 3.18–20, we read:

> For Christ also suffered for sins once for all, the righteous for the unrighteous, in order to bring you to God. He was put to

death in the flesh, but made alive in the spirit, in which also he went and made a proclamation to the spirits in prison, who in former times did not obey, when God waited patiently in the days of Noah, during the building of the ark, in which a few, that is, eight people, were saved through water.

This idea is picked up in the Apostles' Creed where we say, 'he descended to the dead'. This is the lowest point on the movement of salvation. From the dead Jesus is raised, and finally he ascends to heaven, to be seated on the right hand of the Father.

In his Ascension and exaltation God affirms all that Jesus has done through his incarnation, life, death, dealing with hell and resurrection.

In particular the Ascension affirms the resurrection, and shows how it differs from other resurrections that we read of in the Bible, for example, that of Lazarus in John 11. Lazarus rose, only to die again. But by his Ascension to heaven, Jesus has affirmed that his resurrection body will not die; in it he has overcome death itself.

Dealing with the location problem

Another reason why the Ascension is important is that it takes Jesus physically out of this universe. Had he stayed, he would have been the person everyone who followed him wanted to be near. But because of the limitations of space, only a few thousand could be near at any one time. In the first century there were probably about 180 million people in the world and even if they all had the ability to travel, there was no way they could all meet Jesus. Through the Ascension and giving of the Holy Spirit the focus of Christianity moved from the physical presence of Jesus on earth to the witness about him, which could be taken everywhere by his followers.

Why on Earth did it Happen?

Receiving gifts – the gift of the Holy Spirit

The coming of the Holy Spirit is intimately connected with the Ascension. In John 16 Jesus promised that if he left his disciples, he would send the Holy Spirit to them, and in Acts 2.33 Peter tells his hearers that this has indeed happened. The sign to Jesus' disciples that he has gone in triumph into heaven and is exalted is that his Spirit has come to them on earth.

The Holy Spirit is the vital connection between the Head of the body of Christ, which is Jesus the human in heaven, and the rest of the body, his Church on earth. It is the Holy Spirit who gives to the Church the gifts it needs to fulfil its commission. Thus Paul says in Ephesians 4, 'When he ascended on high he made captivity itself a captive; he gave gifts to his people ... The gifts he gave were that some would be apostles, some prophets, some evangelists, some pastors and teachers, to equip the saints for the work of ministry, for building up the body of Christ' (Ephesians 4.8, 11–12).

The Church as Jesus' place on earth

While people look to Pentecost, the giving of the Holy Spirit, as the birth of the Church, we can see that it is Christ's Ascension that led to Pentecost, and so the start of the Church is as much in the Ascension as in Pentecost.

With the Ascension Christ entered into his kingdom and so began a new age in the history of the world. This history can be seen as divided into three ages:

(a) The time of Israel until the coming of John the Baptist
(b) The time of Jesus on earth from the coming of John the Baptist to the Ascension
(c) The time of the Church from the Ascension until Jesus' return.

Jesus is at God's right hand in heaven and is reigning there. But his influence is felt on earth through the Holy Spirit, and in the community of the Church. It is the presence of the Holy Spirit in the Church that provides the link between the real presence of Jesus in heaven, who is thus absent from earth, and the real presence of Jesus in the Church. The Church is not to be confused with Jesus' resurrection body – no, that is in heaven – but it is his continuing expression of himself in history and so in that sense it is his body on earth. The current time is the age of the Church, where God is working to bring in his kingdom on earth in and through the Church.

One who intercedes for us

As we have seen, Jesus in heaven is our great High Priest offering his life to God the Father as the way to restore the relationship between God and humanity. This impacts our prayers on earth. We pray in the power of the Holy Spirit, who is sent by God the Father and the Son, through the Son to God the Father. We are given confidence by Jesus, as the author of Hebrews says:

> Therefore, my friends, since we have confidence to enter the sanctuary by the blood of Jesus, by the new and living way that he opened for us through the curtain (that is, through his flesh), and since we have a great priest over the house of God, let us approach with a true heart in full assurance of faith, with our hearts sprinkled clean from an evil conscience and our bodies washed with pure water. (Hebrews 10.19–22)

We know Jesus is interceding for us, enabling us to come spiritually into heaven by our prayers.

Citizens of heaven

Jesus' presence in heaven is a comfort to us on earth. Just as the Holy Spirit is a pledge of our future with God (2 Corinthians 1.22; 5.5), so also the presence of Jesus, an embodied human, in heaven is a pledge that our humanity is able to come before God.

This gives us citizenship of heaven now. As Paul in Colossians says, 'So if you have been raised with Christ, seek the things that are above, where Christ is, seated at the right hand of God. Set your minds on things that are above, not on things that are on earth' (Colossians 3.1–2).

But in the heart of this is a paradox. For as we set our minds on God and his desires, we find that he points us back to earth and the fulfilment of his mission here. We find grace and power in our relationship with God so that we are empowered to live and work to his praise and glory here on earth. And as we rejoice in being citizens of heaven, we play our part, by the inspiration of the Holy Spirit, in bringing the Kingdom of God closer here on earth.

9

What the First Theologians Wrote about the Ascension

What did the early Church make of the Ascension? How did they use it in their teaching? We know some of this from the letters that were written.

The Ascension and worship in the early Church

The Ascension was not celebrated as a separate festival on the fortieth day after Easter until the fifth century. In the early Christian centuries, the 50 days from Easter Day to Pentecost were one long festival, which celebrated Jesus' death, his resurrection, his Ascension and the coming of the Holy Spirit. All parts of these events interwove in a festival of joy.

In the third century the last day of Pentecost became a particular focus of celebration but it wasn't until the late fourth century that a separate festival of the Ascension developed. When it developed it was at first on the fiftieth day of the Paschal Festival – the day now celebrated as Pentecost.

'The Doctrine of the Apostles', which was written in Syriac and dates to about AD 350, tells of the Ascension and the coming of the Holy Spirit on the same day and then gives rules that the apostles laid down, including this: '9. The apostles further appointed: At the completion of fifty days after His resurrection make ye a commemoration of His ascension to His glorious Father.'

This was the festival that Etheria experienced when she visited Jerusalem in the 380s and recorded what happened there in 'The Pilgrimage of Etheria'.

What the First Theologians Wrote about the Ascension

1. *Whitsunday*
(*a*) *Morning Station.*
But on the fiftieth day, that is, the Lord's Day, when the people have a very great deal to go through, everything that is customary is done from the first cockcrow onwards ...
(*b*) *Station at Sion.*
And when the dismissal has been made at the martyrium, all the people, to a man, escort the bishop with hymns to Sion, [so that] they are in Sion when the third hour is fully come. And on their arrival there the passage from the Acts of the Apostles 2 is read where the Spirit came down so that all tongues [were heard and all men] understood the things that were being spoken ...
(*c*) *Station at the Mount of Olives.*
So all the people return, each to his house, to rest themselves, and immediately after breakfast they ascend the Mount of Olives, that is, to Eleona, each as he can, so that there is no Christian left in the city who does not go. When, therefore, they have gone up the Mount of Olives, that is, to Eleona, they first enter the Imbomon, that is, the place whence the Lord ascended into heaven, and the bishops and the priests take their seat there, and likewise all the people. Lessons are read there with hymns interspersed, antiphons too are said suitable to the day and the place, also the prayers which are interspersed have likewise similar references. The passage from the Gospel is also read where it speaks of the Lord's Ascension, also that from the Acts of the Apostles which tells of the Ascension of the Lord into heaven after His Resurrection.

After this there was also an evening celebration.

This liturgical practice shows a tradition where the Ascension occurred early and unseen, before the coming of the Holy Spirit, and the farewell on the Mount of Olives was a separate event.

However, the celebration of the Ascension as a distinct festival had developed by the time of St John Chrysostom (c. 349–407) and Gregory of Nyssa (c. 335 – after 394), who both refer to it. Augustine says that the Ascension is one of the annual commemorations of the church, recognized everywhere.

The Missing Ending

As to those other things which we hold on the authority, not of Scripture, but of tradition, and which are observed throughout the whole world, it may be understood that they are held as approved and instituted either by the apostles themselves, or by plenary Councils, whose authority in the Church is most useful, *e.g.* the annual commemoration, by special solemnities, of the Lord's passion, resurrection, and ascension, and of the descent of the Holy Spirit from heaven, and whatever else is in like manner observed by the whole Church wherever it has been established. (Augustine, Letter 54, chapter 1)

The Ascension up to the Council of Nicaea (AD 325)

The earliest writings after the New Testament are called the works of the Apostolic Fathers. These were written by church leaders in the late first and very early second centuries. In fact, there is overlap between the dates of these writings and those that were accepted by the Church as part of the Bible. These writings were seen as useful, but not to be in part of the official Bible, since they were not written by an apostle, or at least with the authority of an apostle. There are references to the Ascension in the earliest writings of the Church, but usually it is implied rather than spoken of directly. When the writer speaks of Jesus' expected return or his high priesthood, his presence now in heaven and so his entry there (the Ascension), is implied.

There are three explicit references to the Ascension in this period.

- Ignatius (d. c. 117) wrote to the Magnesians: '7.2 Do ye therefore all come together as unto the temple of God, as unto one altar, as unto one Jesus Christ, who came forth from one Father, and lived in one, and departed unto one.'
- The Epistle of Barnabas (c. 120) has: '15.9 Wherefore we keep the eighth day as a day of gladness, on which also Jesus rose from the dead, and after he had appeared ascended unto heaven.'

What the First Theologians Wrote about the Ascension

- Also, Polycarp, a second-century Bishop of Smyrna, in what is now Turkey, wrote to the Philippians:

  > 2.1 Wherefore gird up your loins and serve God in fear and truth, forsaking the vain and empty talking and the error of the many, for that ye have believed on Him that raised our Lord Jesus Christ from the dead and gave unto him glory and a throne on His right hand.

These writings tell us that the Ascension was accepted as a fact at this early stage; indeed, it was seen by Polycarp as part of the basic statements about the faith. The Epistle of Barnabas suggests that it happened on Easter Day.

The next group of writers are now known as the second-century Apologists. They wrote to defend Christianity from rumours that were circulating at the time and to show that the belief in many gods (polytheism) was incorrect. They wrote to the state authorities in legal documents asking for the reality of Christianity to be investigated. Because of this they are using arguments from reason and so say little on the Ascension. The Apology of Aristides (c. AD 143) does refer to the Ascension as a fact: 'And he died and was buried; and they say that after three days he rose and ascended to heaven.' But here again there is no attempt to draw out further ideas from this.

Justin Martyr

By the time of Justin (d. c. 165) the idea of the Ascension itself is under attack, and so we start to get more written about it. He often summarizes the key teaching of Christianity, and in these summaries the Ascension has its place. So, we read, 'The Word, who is the first-birth of God, was produced without sexual union, and that He, Jesus Christ, our Teacher, was crucified and died, and rose again, and ascended into heaven' (Justin Martyr, *The First Apology Of Justin*, chapter 21). Similar words appear in his *First Apology* at sections 31, 42, 46 and in Justin's *Dialogue with Trypho* at 63, 85, 126 and 132.

Clearly the creed is beginning to be developed.

The Missing Ending

But Justin does more than refer to these events, he seeks to defend them. So, in his *First Apology*, chapter 21 he goes on:

> For you know how many sons your esteemed writers ascribed to Jupiter: Mercury, the interpreting word and teacher of all; Aesculapius, who, though he was a great physician, was struck by a thunderbolt, and so ascended to heaven; and Bacchus too, after he had been torn limb from limb; and Hercules, when he had committed himself to the flames to escape his toils; and the sons of Leda, and Dioscuri; and Perseus, son of Danae; and Bellerophon, who, though sprung from mortals, rose to heaven on the horse Pegasus.

Whatever we may think of the historicity, or lack of it, of these, in his time Justin used these tales to show his readers that the idea of a man rising to heaven was not far-fetched.

Justin also used the Psalms in his dealing with the Ascension. He quotes Psalm 110.1–3 in his *First Apology*, chapter 45:

> And that God the Father of all would bring Christ to heaven after He had raised Him from the dead, and would keep Him there until He has subdued His enemies the devils, and until the number of those who are foreknown by Him as good and virtuous is complete, on whose account He has still delayed the consummation – hear what was said by the prophet David. These are his words: 'The Lord said unto My Lord, Sit Thou at My right hand, until I make Thine enemies Thy footstool. The Lord shall send to Thee the rod of power out of Jerusalem; and rule Thou in the midst of Thine enemies. With Thee is the government in the day of Thy power, in the beauties of Thy saints: from the womb of morning have I begotten Thee.

In his *Dialogue with Trypho*, chapter 32, he says,

> and that the Lord, the Father of all, has brought Him again from the earth, setting Him at His own right hand, until He makes His enemies His footstool; which indeed happens from

What the First Theologians Wrote about the Ascension

the time that our Lord Jesus Christ ascended to heaven, after He rose again from the dead, the times now running on to their consummation.

He goes on in chapter 33 to argue that Psalm 110 points to Jesus as a priest in the order of Melchizedek.
In chapter 39 he refers to Psalm 68:

> Listen, O friend, for I am not mad or beside myself; but it was prophesied that, after the ascent of Christ to heaven, He would deliver us from error and give us gifts. The words are these: 'He ascended up on high; He led captivity captive; He gave gifts to men.' Accordingly, we who have received gifts from Christ, who has ascended up on high, prove from the words of prophecy that you, 'the wise in yourselves, and the men of understanding in your own eyes,' are foolish, and honour God and His Christ by lip only.

He goes on to link the Ascension with the gift of wisdom by the Holy Spirit.
Justin Martyr also links Psalms 19, 24 and 47 to the Ascension.

Irenaeus

Irenaeus (c. 130–200) was the bishop of the Greek-speaking community in Lyons. He was perhaps the first theologian to really work on the idea of the Ascension. He was writing at a time when some were suggesting that the physical and the spiritual don't really mix. His main target was the teaching of Valentius, who taught that the Primal Being had produced other beings called aeons, which through their errors produced matter. So, the material could not hope to come to God, but only the spiritual. Such teaching is known as gnosticism, since only some could hope to spiritually reach God and they did this through having special knowledge (the Greek for 'knowledge' is *gnosis*). Valentius and others were attracted to such ideas as a way of making Christianity more like the ideas of Platonism,

The Missing Ending

which saw a divide between the remote 'One' and the earthly. Against this teaching Irenaeus sets the physical Ascension of Jesus into heaven.

> [The Church believes] in one God, the Father Almighty, Maker of heaven, and earth, and the sea, and all things that are in them; and in one Christ Jesus, the Son of God, who became incarnate for our salvation; and in the Holy Spirit, who proclaimed through the prophets the dispensations of God, and the advents, and the birth from a virgin, and the passion, and the resurrection from the dead, and the ascension into heaven in the flesh of the beloved Christ Jesus. (*Against the Heresies*, Book 1, 10.1)

Irenaeus is quoting the creed as he has received it, but he emphasizes that Jesus' Ascension is 'in the flesh' since that is relevant to his argument.

The key idea of Irenaeus' thinking is 'recapitulation' of human life in Jesus. Jesus comes as a second Adam, a second representative human. He lives a fully human life and faces the same temptations, but this time the 'human' is obedient, and so the outcome is different. Adam's disobedience led to humanity being enslaved by the devil; Jesus' obedience led to the enslavement of the devil.

This recapitulation is completed when Jesus ascended taking captivity captive:

> For the Lord, through means of suffering, 'ascending into the lofty place, led captivity captive, gave gifts to men,' and conferred on those that believe in Him the power 'to tread upon serpents and scorpions, and on all the power of the enemy,' that is, of the leader of apostasy. (*Against the Heresies*, Book 2, 20.3)

Irenaeus links Jesus' Ascension to his suffering, a real suffering, unlike the way in which his opponents reckoned that Jesus only seemed to be physical, and so did not really suffer.

The other aspect of recapitulation for Irenaeus is that Jesus 'sums up' humanity in himself. So what happened for him happens for us. His Ascension into heaven in the flesh enables us to come before God in our time.

> Himself becoming the first begotten of the dead, and in Himself raising up man that was fallen, lifting him up far above the heaven to the right hand of the glory of the Father: even as God promised by the prophet, saying: And I will raise up the tabernacle of David that is fallen; that is, the flesh that was from David. And this our Lord Jesus Christ truly fulfilled, when He gloriously achieved our redemption, that He might truly raise us up, setting us free unto the Father. (*Demonstration of the Apostolic Preaching* 38)

The key for Irenaeus was that he let what he knew of Jesus, and what he had done, take precedence in his thinking over what people were saying about the way the universe is, and their philosophical ideas of how the world ought to be.

Tertullian

Tertullian (c. 160–c. 220), who lived in Carthage in the Roman province of Africa and wrote in Latin, used the Ascension as one of his tools in dealing with the heretical ideas he was confronting. When he is talking about baptism he uses the Ascension to show that the difference between the baptism of John the Baptist and Christian baptism is the gift of the Holy Spirit.

> Even the Lord Himself said that the Spirit would not descend on any other condition, but that He should first ascend to the Father. What the Lord was not yet conferring, of course the servant could not furnish. Accordingly, in the Acts of the Apostles, we find that men who had 'John's baptism' had not received the Holy Spirit, whom they knew not even by hearing. (*On Baptism* 10)

Tertullian is also opposed to the docetists, who claimed that Jesus was never really a physical human being, but a spiritual being that took on the appearance of human flesh. Tertullian used the Ascension of Jesus as a physical human to help in this confrontation.

> Jesus is still sitting there at the right hand of the Father, man, yet God – the last Adam, yet the primary Word – flesh and blood, yet purer than ours – who 'shall descend in like manner as He ascended *into heaven*' the same both in substance and form, as the angels affirmed, so as even to be recognised by those who pierced Him. Designated, as He is, 'the Mediator' between God and man, He keeps in His own self the deposit of the flesh which has been committed to Him by both parties – the pledge and security of its entire perfection. For as 'He has given to us the earnest of the Spirit,' so has He received from us the earnest of the flesh, and has carried it with Him into heaven as a pledge of that complete entirety which is one day to be restored to it. Be not disquieted, O flesh and blood, with any care; in Christ you have acquired both heaven and the kingdom of God. (*On the Resurrection of the Flesh* 51)

So, for Tertullian the presence of Jesus in heaven is a guarantee that our flesh will be there one day. There is a symmetry between us receiving the Holy Spirit from heaven and human flesh, in Jesus' humanity, going into heaven, and both give us security that we, as real, enfleshed humans, will come before God and be accepted by him.

Tertullian also talks of Jesus creating an entrance to heaven for us by his Ascension:

> Know that both that way of ascent was thereafter levelled with the ground, by the footsteps of the Lord, and an entrance thereafter opened up by the might of Christ, and that no delay or inquest will meet Christians on the threshold, since they have there to be not discriminated from one another, but owned, and not put to the question, but received in. For though you think heaven still shut, remember that the Lord left here to Peter and through him to the Church, the keys of it, which every one who has been here put to the question, and also made confession, will carry with him. (*Scorpiace* 10)

What the First Theologians Wrote about the Ascension

One further faulty idea that Tertullian had to deal with was the idea that God the Father was himself born and suffered – that the Father was Jesus Christ. This is attractive to those who find the idea of God in three persons difficult. For them it is easier to think of God being first the Father, then Jesus and then the Holy Spirit. This heresy is called 'patripassianism', from the Latin for 'Father', *patri* and 'suffer', *passio*, or 'modalism' from the different mode which God is thought be in at each stage. To correct this idea Tertullian wrote:

> It is the Son, too, who ascends to the heights of heaven, and also descends to the inner parts of the earth. He sitteth at the Father's right hand – not the Father at His own. He is seen by Stephen, at his martyrdom by stoning, still sitting at the right hand of where He will continue to sit, until the Father shall make His enemies His footstool. (*Against Praxeus* 30)

The idea of God being by turns Father, Son and Holy Spirit is clearly seen to be a nonsense whenever more than one person of the Trinity is seen interacting with another. Jesus sitting at God's right hand was one of the more graphic cases which Tertullian could draw on.

Hippolytus

Hippolytus (d. 235) lived in Rome and wrote a book in Latin to deal with the heresies he knew of at the time, *Against all the Heresies*. One heresy he was dealing with was that of Noetus who was modalist, that is, he believed that God was in turn the Father, then the Son, then the Holy Spirit.

> He Himself attests it who came down from heaven; for He speaketh thus: 'No man hath ascended up to heaven, but He that came down from heaven, even the Son of man which is in heaven.' What then can he [that is Noetus] seek beside what is thus written?
>
> Will he say, forsooth, that flesh was in heaven? Yet there is the flesh which was presented by the Father's Word as an

offering, – the flesh that came by the Spirit and the Virgin, (and was) demonstrated to be the perfect Son of God. It is evident, therefore, that He offered Himself to the Father. And before this there was no flesh in heaven. Who, then, was in heaven but the Word unincarnate, who was despatched to show that He was upon earth and was also in heaven? (*Against Noetus* 4)

Hippolytus' argument is that in John 3 we hear that only the man who descended from heaven has gone up into heaven. But there was no human flesh, no human body in heaven before the Son of God was born of a human woman. Yet he returned to heaven with his human flesh and offered it to God the Father. This means that God the Son cannot be the same as God the Father, while they are still both God.

Novatian

Novatian (d. 258) also lived in Rome and is remembered for setting himself up as a rival pope to Cornelius who he felt was too lenient with those who buckled under the persecution led by Emperor Decius. Before this he was a well-regarded theologian. Among his works was *On the Trinity*. When discussing Christ, Novatian refers to the Ascension to show that Jesus is human and also completely divine.

> And in the same manner as He ascended as man into heaven, so as God He had first descended thence. And in the same manner as He goes as man to the Father, so as the Son in obedience to the Father He shall descend thence. (*On the Trinity* 11)

Cyprian

Cyprian (d. 258) was a Bishop of Carthage in north Africa and in the next generation was also contending against wrong ideas of Christianity. However, the issues were more to do with how to deal with people who had caved in under persecution, rather than on matters of doctrine as such. He does use the Ascension in his work *On the Unity of the Church* to encourage a confessor to show humility:

> He is a confessor, let him be lowly and quiet; let him be in his doings modest with discipline, so that he who is called a confessor of Christ may imitate Christ whom he confesses. For since He says, 'Whosoever exalteth himself shall be abased, and he who humbleth himself shall be exalted;' and since He Himself has been exalted by the Father, because as the Word, and the strength, and the wisdom of God the Father, He humbled Himself upon earth, how can He love arrogance, who even by His own law enjoined upon us humility, and Himself received the highest name from the Father as the reward of His humility? (*On the Unity of the Church* 21)

Jesus chose to be humbled, and was rewarded with being exalted. So those who serve him should seek humility, knowing that they too will be exalted with Jesus because of his Ascension.

Origen

Origen (d. 254) lived and wrote in Alexandria in Egypt. He was interested in showing that you could hold the current philosophy of Platonism and be a Christian. In *On First Principles*, the descent/ascent theme runs through it all, but for Origen descent is about Jesus becoming material and ascent about leaving behind what belongs to our present physical existence, so perhaps the ideas of Plato win out over the Christian ideas at this point.

This means that Origen tends to interpret the Ascension as a movement of the mind, rather than a physical event. So, in his book *On Prayer* he says, 'Let ours be the more reverent conception of the ascension of the Son to the Father with sanctified insight, an ascension rather of soul than of body' (*On Prayer* 13). This does not mean that Origen did not believe in the Ascension; he refers to it in several places, including:

We also have 'a great High Priest,' who by the greatness of His power and understanding 'has passed through the heavens, even Jesus the Son of God,' who has promised to all that have truly learned divine things, and have lived lives in harmony with them, to go before them to the things that are supra-mundane; for His words are: 'That where I go, ye may be also.' (*Against Celsius* 6.20)

He believes in a real, but spiritual, Ascension. He downplays the body of Jesus in the Ascension, favouring the idea of his soul returning to God. Origen saw as important the fact that God cannot be said to be in one place rather than another, and so God the Son cannot move in space when he descends to earth and ascends to heaven. So he saw the Ascension as a spiritual exaltation rather than a physical movement.

> But these words about the coming of the Father and the Son to him who loves the word of Jesus do not mean a coming to a place, nor should they be taken as referring to a place. The Word of God in coming down to dwell with us and, considering his own proper dignity, humbling Himself while He is among men, is said to pass out of the world to the Father, so that we too may contemplate him there in His perfection, when he returns from the emptiness wherewith he emptied himself among us to His own fullness. And we too, if we follow Him as guide, will there receive fullness and be delivered from all our emptiness. (*Prayer in Exhortation to Martyrdom*)

Origen links the coming of the Holy Spirit to the Ascension in his *On First Principles*: 'I observe, however, that the chief advent of the Holy Spirit is declared to men, after the ascension of Christ to heaven, rather than before His coming into the world' (2.7.2).

Methodius

Methodius (d. 311), who was probably Bishop of Philippi in Greece, opposed Origen's 'spiritualization' of the resurrection and the Ascension. He therefore emphasizes the physical nature of the Ascension in his *Symposium* (which is written in a style that imitates Plato, but does not agree with his philosophy), referring to 'The undefiled and blessed flesh, which the Word Himself carried into the heavens, and presented at the right hand of God' (*The Symposium* 7.8).

So, in this period the references to the Ascension show that it was accepted as an important part of the developing creed, but most thinkers go little further than that. Irenaeus is the first to really reflect on the doctrine of the Ascension and sees it as the completion of Jesus' 'recapitulation' or reworking and summing up human life. Origen then takes the idea in a different direction by arguing for a spiritual Ascension of Christ, rather than a movement of a human body from earth to heaven.

The Ascension from Nicaea

In AD 313 Constantine and Licinius, emperors of the Western and Eastern parts of the Roman Empire, visited Milan to celebrate the marriage of Constantia, Constantine's half-sister, to Licinius. While there, they issued the Edict of Milan which gave toleration to Christians and to other worshippers of 'whatever heavenly deity exists'. This edict affirmed the edict issued in 311 by Emperor Galerius as he was dying, which gave toleration to Christians. David Edwards (Edwards, 1997, p. 71) suggests that five million out of the 60 million people in the Roman Empire were now Christians.

Constantine went beyond toleration for Christians; he used tax money to pay for churches to be built on key sites in Israel. He also began the Christianization of the empire: law courts were closed on Sunday, he forbade crucifixion, and the cross began to be the public symbol of Christianity. He decided that the empire would be best served by having one religion, and wanted the time when dissent existed within the Church to be at an end. So, he became interested in the resolution of disputes within Christianity.

But what was true Christianity, when there were groups that

followed different leaders and promoted different ideas? The way to resolve this was to get together the bishops from the whole Roman Empire to work out a statement of what was 'orthodox' Christianity.

In 325 the bishops gathered at Nicaea, which is now Iznik in Turkey. This council is called the First Ecumenical Council of the Church, since it was the first attempt to get together bishops from everywhere ('ecumenical' comes from the Greek word *oikoumene*, which means the whole inhabited world; in fact most of the bishops came from the Greek East of the empire, with only five from the Latin-speaking West). In the following centuries there were to be six further such councils, the last being at Nicaea in AD 787. After this the tensions between the churches in the West and in the East became too great, and the political powers too weak, to ensure future gatherings from the whole Church.

The big dispute that the first gathering at Nicaea was to resolve was between those who agreed with Arius and those who agreed with Athanasius, about the nature of Jesus.

Athanasius

Athanasius (d. 373) was the Bishop of Alexandria and Arius was one of his presbyters. Arius argued that Jesus was not God himself, but the chief of God's creatures; he was like God but not of the same substance as God. Athanasius responded that if Jesus was not God in himself, being of the same substance, it was a creature who died on the cross, and so his death could not have the universal effect that Christians believe Jesus' death has for us.

Among many other doctrines pressed into service on each side was the Ascension.

The Arians argued that Jesus was clearly seen as lower than God in the Bible. For example, in Philippians 2.9 we read that Jesus was exalted. To be exalted means that you were inferior before this. We only know what the Arians argued because we have Athanasius' reply. In his *Against the Arians* I.40, Athanasius quotes Philippians 2.5–11 and then refutes the idea that Jesus in his essence was promoted by God; rather, having humbled himself he was restored. The Arians also used Acts 2.36, where Peter affirms that God made Jesus 'both Lord and Christ', to argue that Jesus only began to be Lord after his Ascension. Athanasius uses the Ascension in response to this:

> For if, being God, He became man, and descending from on high He is still said to be exalted, where is He exalted, being God? This withal being plain, that, since God is highest of all, His Word must necessarily be highest also ... the term in question, 'highly exalted,' does not signify that the essence of the Word was exalted, for He was ever and is 'equal to God' but the exaltation is of the manhood ... Since then the Word, being the Image of the Father and immortal, took the form of the servant, and as man underwent for us death in His flesh, that thereby He might offer Himself for us through death to the Father; therefore also, as man, He is said because of us and for us to be highly exalted, that as by His death we all died in Christ, so again in the Christ Himself we might be highly exalted, being raised from the dead, and ascending into heaven, 'whither the forerunner Jesus is for us entered, not into the figures of the true, but into heaven itself, now to appear in the presence of God for us'. But if now for us the Christ is entered into heaven itself, though He was even before and always Lord and Framer of the heavens, for us therefore is that present exaltation written. And as He Himself, who sanctifies all, says also that He sanctifies Himself to the Father for our sakes, not that the Word may become holy, but that He Himself may in Himself sanctify all of us (*Against the Arians* I.40–41)

His argument is that as the Son of God, as the Word, Jesus was always equal to God the Father, and so did not need to be exalted. But when he became human, he took the humility of bearing our human flesh. So, it was as a human he was exalted to the Father. As the Son of God he did not need to be exalted, but by being exalted as a human he has made a way for us, who are humans and who have been joined to him, to be exalted to God.

But perhaps the most important thing Athanasius did for the doctrine of the Ascension was to ensure that it had its place in the Nicene Creed, for he was part of the Council of Nicaea which wrote this:

> On the third day he rose again
> in accordance with the Scriptures;
> he ascended into heaven
> and is seated at the right hand of the Father.

Eusebius of Caesarea

Eusebius (d. 339) was a Greek Palestinian bishop of Caesarea Maritima on the Mediterranean coast of the Holy Land who is best known as the first church historian. He echoes Origen's views when he discusses the Ascension in his *Proof of the Gospel*: 'And when there is a fit opportunity I will shew that we must understand the Descent and Ascension of God the Word not as of one moving locally, but in the metaphorical sense which Scripture intends in the use of such conventional terms' (*Proof of the Gospel* 9).

Hilary of Poitiers

Hilary (d. c. 368) was a bishop in what is now western France and was involved in defending the Nicaean agreement against Arians in the West. In his *On the Trinity* he links the nature of Jesus as both God and man to the Ascension. He was one of those who spoke of God the Son emptying himself of his divine form so that he could take the servant's form as a human. This emptying led to there being an infinite distance between God the Son united to a human nature and God the Father, which was only overcome at the Ascension, when Jesus' human nature was exalted to the presence of God.

> He emptied Himself of the form of God and took the form of a servant, when He was born. But the Father's nature, with which He was in natural unity, was not affected by this

assumption of flesh; ... For the object to be gained was that man might become God. But the assumed manhood could not in any wise abide in the unity of God, unless, through unity with God, it attained to unity with the nature of God. ... Therefore the Father must reinstate the Word in His unity, that the offspring of His nature might again return to be glorified in Himself: for the unity had been infringed by the new dispensation, and could only be restored perfect as before if the Father glorified with Himself the flesh assumed by the Son. (*On the Trinity* 9.38)

Since Jesus united human nature to the divine and was exalted to God, with both natures, our humanity has been reconciled to God and we may come before him.

He is but One, one Jesus Christ for us, Son of God and Son of Man, God the Word and Man in the flesh, Who suffered, died, was buried, rose again, was received into heaven, and sits at the right hand of God: Who possesses in His one single self, according to the Divine Plan and nature, in the form of God and in the form of a servant, the Human and Divine without separation or division. (*On the Trinity* 10.65)

For Hilary the Ascension affects all people. When he is commenting on 'a city set on a hill' in Matthew 5.14 he calls Jesus' human flesh a 'city', since there are many of us who share in the same humanity as Jesus. This city is now in the heights through the Ascension.

He calls the flesh which he had assumed 'a city', because as a city is formed of a variety and multitude of inhabitants, so in Him, through the nature of the body which He had taken on Himself, an assembling together so to speak, of the whole human race is contained ... Therefore it cannot now be hid because it has been placed in the heights of the most exalted God and has been lifted up to the wonder of His works to be contemplated and understood by all. (*Commentary on Matthew*)

The Missing Ending

This passage illustrates the way in which the early Church teachers used allegory in their interpretation of the Bible. They would take a passage and as well as any surface meaning would look for ways in which what is written could illustrate other aspects of the Christian faith.

Ambrose of Milan

Ambrose (d. 397) was another who stood up to the Arians in the West. He uses the Ascension as part of his defence of Jesus' nature as fully God. He also says that the coming of the Spirit depended on the Ascension:

> Be thy gates lifted up, then, that Christ may come in unto thee, not such a Christ as the Arians take Him to be – petty, and weak, and menial – but Christ in the form of God, Christ with the Father; that He may enter such as He is, exalted above the heaven and all things; and that He may send forth upon thee His Holy Spirit. It is expedient for thee that thou shouldst believe that He hath ascended and is sitting at the right hand of the Father, for if in impious thought thou detain Him amongst things created and earthly, if He depart not for thee, ascend not for thee, then to thee the Comforter shall not come, even as Christ Himself hath told us: 'For if I go not away, the Comforter will not come unto you, but if I depart, I will send Him unto you.' (*Exposition of the Faith* 4.24)

Ambrose also sees Jesus as the one who opens the way to God for us. In becoming human 'he took us in that flesh'. Hence, 'His death is our death: His Resurrection our resurrection, and his Ascension our Ascension, "for it was not merely one man but the whole world that entered in the Person of the All-Redeemer"' (*Exposition of the Faith* 4.7).

Cyril of Jerusalem

Cyril (d. 386) gave a series of lectures in which he looked at the truths of the faith. Lecture 14 was given the day after he had

What the First Theologians Wrote about the Ascension

preached on the Ascension, and he refers back to that sermon in the lecture. He sees the Ascension as the fulfilment of Old Testament prophecy, pointing to Psalms 24, 47 and 68 and also Amos 9.6. But he distinguishes the Ascension from the assumptions of Enoch and Elijah. In particular,

> That Elias said that a double portion in the Holy Spirit should be given to his holy disciple; but that Christ granted to His own disciples so great enjoyment of the grace of the Holy Ghost, as not only to have It in themselves, but also, by the laying on of their hands, to impart the fellowship of It to them who believed. (Catechetical Lecture 14)

So, Jesus' Ascension is very much greater than the assumptions of Elijah or Moses since he sends the Holy Spirit not just on one disciple but on many, and they in turn can lay hands on others and pass the Holy Spirit on. The results of Jesus' Ascension are of a different order of magnitude from the results of Elijah's assumption, and so his Ascension itself must be different.

Gregory of Nazianzus

Gregory of Nazianzus (d. c. 389), a Greek-speaking bishop in what is now central Turkey, was more interested in our being able to reach and relate to God than in the details of the Ascension. So, he writes:

> The result will be that you will abandon these carnal and grovelling doctrines, and learn to be more sublime, and to ascend with His Godhead, and you will not remain permanently among the things of sight, but will rise up with Him into the world of thought, and come to know which passages refer to His Nature, and which His assumption of Human Nature. (*The Third Theological Oration. On the Son* 18)

The first sermons

As the Church became settled as the religion of the Roman Empire the Church's calendar began to be worked out. This meant that different events in the history of our redemption were remembered and celebrated at different times of the year. Once the Festival of the Ascension was being celebrated as a distinct festival, preachers began to write sermons, which were copied and kept.

Early out of the blocks were both Gregory of Nyssa and John Chrysostom.

Gregory of Nyssa

Gregory of Nyssa (d. c. 394), another bishop of what is now central Turkey and friends with the other Gregory, quotes Psalms 24 and 68 and goes along with those before him in seeing them as prefiguring the Ascension in a sermon that he preached as Bishop of Nyssa. But it is in the rest of Gregory's writings that we really see his ideas about the Ascension – in his sermon he re-trod old ground. Gregory affirms that the exaltation of Jesus refers to his humanity:

> Paul also says that He was 'highly exalted' after the Passion and the Resurrection, not being exalted in so far forth as He is God. For what height is there more sublime than the Divine height, that he should say God was exalted thereunto? But he means that the lowliness of the Humanity was exalted, the word, I suppose, indicating the assimilation and union of the Man Who was assumed to the exalted state of the Divine Nature. (*Against Eunomius* 6.4)

Later, while pondering Jesus' words to Mary Magdalene in the garden in John 20, he makes clear that God cannot move through space, so the movement seen in the Ascension has to refer to Jesus' human body:

What the First Theologians Wrote about the Ascension

> He Who says, 'I go,' indicates local change, while He who contains all things, 'in Whom,' as the Apostle says, 'all things were created, and in Whom all things consist' has nothing in existent things external to Himself to which removal could take place by any kind of motion, (for motion cannot otherwise be effected than by that which is removed leaving the place in which it is, and occupying another place instead, while that which extends through all, and is in all, and controls all, and is confined by no existent thing, has no place to which to pass, inasmuch as nothing is void of the Divine fulness). (*Against Eunomius* 12.1)

He also sees the exaltation of Jesus' body as a sign that we too will be brought to God our Father. He uses the image of the first fruits:

> For that which has taken place in Christ's humanity is a common boon bestowed on mankind generally. For as when we see in Him the weight of the body, which naturally gravitates to earth, ascending through the air into the heavens, we believe according to the words of the Apostle, that we also 'shall be caught up in the clouds to meet the Lord in the air,' even so, when we hear that the true God and Father has become the God and Father of our First-fruits, we no longer doubt that the same God has become our God and Father too, inasmuch as we have learnt that we shall come to the same place whither Christ has entered for us as our forerunner. (*Against Eunomius* 12.1)

Gregory's views are not innovative, but he reaffirms the thinking on the Ascension which he has received.

John Chrysostom

John Chrysostom (d. 407) was gaining a reputation as a preacher in Antioch when in AD 392 he preached on the Ascension. He was later to be made Archbishop of Constantinople and was remembered for many years after his life as a great preacher. He adds the use of imagery to the bare ideas about the Ascension.

In his 'Homily on the Ascension', after saying, 'and today is the foundation of these benefits [i.e. our reconciliation with God], for as he assumed the first fruits of our nature, so He took them up to the Lord,' he continues:

> For as it happens in a field full of corn, when a man takes a few ears of corn and makes a small sheaf and offers it to God, he blesses the whole cornfield by means of this sheaf, so Christ has done this also, and through that one flesh and first fruits has made our race to be blessed.

He also explains from Leviticus 19.23, 24 that the first fruits do not need to be the first fruit that is borne by a tree but the first good fruits. This is why the human nature that was offered was that which was freed from sin in Christ, rather than that which came before him.

Like others, he distinguishes between Elijah's assumption and Jesus' Ascension, but he uses different grounds. John Chrysostom notes that Elijah was taken up in a fiery chariot, but Jesus in a cloud.

> For when it was necessary for the servant to be called, a chariot was sent, but when the Son, a royal throne, and not simply a royal throne but the Father's. For concerning the Father Isaiah says: 'Behold, the Lord sitteth upon a light cloud.' Since the Father sits upon a cloud, He sends the cloud for the Son.

In his second 'Homily of the Acts of the Apostles', which he gave in Constantinople, many of the points from the 'Homily on the Ascension' were repeated, but he adds one other point:

> In the Resurrection they saw the end but not the beginning, and in the Ascension they saw the beginning but not the end. Because in the former it had been superfluous to have seen the beginning, the Lord himself who spake these things being present and the sepulchre showing clearly that he was

not there; but in the latter they needed to be informed of the sequel by the words of others.

In this way, Chrysostom explains why the angels needed to appear and tell the disciples that Jesus had gone into heaven.

Chrysostom also distinguishes between an assumption such as Elijah experienced and an ascension such as that of Jesus.

> Moreover the angels did not say: 'whom ye have seen taken up', but 'going into heaven'. Ascension is the word not assumption. The expression 'taken up' belongs to the flesh ... Of the expressions, some are adapted to the conception of the disciples, some agreeable with the divine majesty.

A second sermon on the Ascension is assigned to John Chrysostom but it may not be actually written by him. But whoever wrote the sermon, it has an interesting emphasis on the parallel between Jesus going into heaven with a human body and the Holy Spirit coming to us from heaven. Both are seen as pledges of salvation (just as Tertullian had seen them). The preacher says, 'Above his body, below his Spirit for us.' He then points out that while the Spirit is on earth with us, he is also in heaven, and just so, while Jesus has his human body in heaven, he has also a body on earth in the Church (quoted in Davies, 1958, p. 119).

Augustine of Hippo

Augustine (d. 430), another north African bishop, wrote some of the first sermons in Latin on the Ascension that are still in existence. Augustine's teaching revolves round four points:

(1) his interpretation of John 3.13;
(2) his doctrine of *Christus totus*, that is, the whole Christ, which is the Head and the members, Jesus and the Church;
(3) the nature of the bodily Ascension of Jesus;
(4) the 40 days between the resurrection and the Ascension.

When he is interpreting John 3.13 in his work 'The Agony of Christ', written in about 397, Augustine says, 'The Lord ascended but the body did not ascend, but was raised into heaven, being raised by Him who ascended' (quoted in Davies, 1958, p. 136). He is acknowledging the Ascension, and that Jesus' body went into heaven, but is reluctant to see it as an ascension of his humanity as such.

Augustine also explains his idea of the 'whole Christ'. In this third 'Homily of the Ascension' he encourages his hearers to ascend in their hearts with Christ, recalling Colossians 3.1–2. He then talks of the unity 'by which He is our Head and we are His body. When He ascended into heaven, we were not separated from him.'

He then argues against those who say that Jesus' body cannot have ascended into heaven.

> How, they say, can the body which did not descend from heaven ascend into heaven? But this refers to a Person and not to the bodily appearance of a person. He descended without the covering of a body; He ascended with the covering of a body. (Davies, 1958, p. 137)

In his 91st sermon, Augustine puts it like this: 'Does thou wish to ascend? Hold fast Him who ascended. For thou canst not raise thyself by thyself ... Be a member of Him who alone has ascended. For the Head with the rest of the members is one man.' The body with which Jesus has ascended into heaven is recognized to be different from our earthly bodies. It is

> ... one which has been made subject to spirit in such a wise that it is adapted to heavenly habitation, all frailty and every earthly blemish having been changed and converted into heavenly purity and stability ... but the question as to where and in what manner the Lord's body is in heaven is one which would be altogether over curious and superfluous to prosecute. Only we must believe that it is in heaven. (*On Faith and the Creed*)

Augustine also emphasizes the 40-day period from the resurrection to the Ascension, referring to Moses' time on Sinai and the years the Israelites spent in the desert ('Third Homily on the Ascension').

When reviewing Augustine's writings on the Ascension, Douglas Farrow (1999) notes a movement in his thought from the early writings to the later ones. In his early writings Farrow detects his prior neo-Platonism with its disdain for the material. By the time he wrote *The City of God*, Augustine was affirming that the material is good. However, when we look at how Augustine links the Ascension to the believers' experience Farrow sees a tendency to play down the physical nature of Jesus' body.

In *On the Trinity*, Augustine explains that the Ascension was necessary so that Jesus' human body was no longer seen. While he was seen as a human, people would think him less than God the Father.

> It was necessary, then, that the form of a servant should be taken away from their eyes, because, through gazing upon it, they thought that alone which they saw to be Christ. Hence also is that which is said, If you loved me, you would rejoice because I said, 'I go unto the Father; for my Father is greater than I:' that is, on that account it is necessary for me to go to the Father, because, while you see me thus, you hold me to be less than the Father through that which you see; and so, being taken up with the creature and the fashion which I have taken upon me, you do not perceive the equality which I have with the Father. (*On the Trinity* 1.18)

Augustine's emphasis on 'the whole Christ' plays down Jesus' human nature in heaven, and preferring to see the Church as his continuing incarnation. By neglecting Jesus' heavenly priesthood, his glory and role as mediator are easily transferred to the Church.

Leo the Great

Leo (d. 461) was Bishop of Rome in the fifth century. Unlike most preachers of this time Leo is not concerned with bringing out the meaning of the Scriptures. For him the sermon is part of the celebration of the Christian mysteries that is the liturgy and is about helping the hearers to understand and enter more fully into these (Robinson, 2009, p. 528). So when he preaches he says 'today' of what is being celebrated, as in 'today Christ is born'. In the service what is being celebrated is no longer in the past but is made present for Christians today.

For Leo the Ascension is the culmination of Jesus' redeeming work. He has descended in his incarnation and death; in his resurrection his ascending begins and comes to its conclusion as he takes his human nature into heaven. 'We recall and rightly venerate that day when our lowly nature was carried in Christ above all hosts of heaven, over all angelic orders and beyond the height of all powers, to the seat of God the Father' (Sermon 74.1).

The Ascension also has a future value for us, since 'where the glory of the Head has preceded us, there hope for the body is also invited' (Sermon 73.4). It also makes a difference 'today'.

> Today (*hodie*) we are established not only as possessors of Paradise, but we have even penetrated the heights of the heavens in Christ ... Those whom the violent enemy threw down from the happiness of our first dwelling, the Son of God has placed, incorporated (*concorporatos*) within himself, at the right hand of the Father. (Sermon 73.4)

For Leo, Christ's Ascension does not make him absent from the earth. His humanity is in heaven, but he is present on earth in his divinity. Rather, the Ascension enabled his disciples to see that Jesus is divine and so,

> A more instructed faith (*eruditior fides*) began to give assent to the Son equal to the Father ... because the faith of believers was drawn there, where the only-begotten Son equal to the Father might be touched not by fleshly hand but by the spiritual intellect. (Sermon 74.4)

Robinson explains this:

Christ becomes more present in divinity as he becomes more absent in humanity. On the one hand, the Church is not separated from Christ because human nature has ascended in him to God's right hand. On the other hand, Christ continues to be divinely present on earth, because 'what was to be seen of our Redeemer has passed over into the Sacraments (*quod itaque Redemptoris nostri conspicuum fuit, in sacramenta transmit*). In order that faith might be more perfect and more firm, teaching has taken the place of sight (*visioni doctrina successif*), and to this authority the hearts of believers, illumined by heavenly rays, have conformed.' It should be remembered that Leo typically uses the word *sacramentum* with reference to the mysteries of the saving acts of Christ, which are celebrated and experienced anew in the Church's worship throughout the liturgical year. (2009, p. 533)

From the First Sermons to the Reformation

While the first century after the inclusion of a separate Ascension Day celebration saw many sermons on the subject, little of significance was written about the Ascension for the next millennium. It was upheld as an article of faith, but thoughts on the subject were confined to what had been written before. In the Eastern church the same view was held on all matters of doctrine. By the Sixth General Council in 680 all that needed to be said had been said, so the work of later generations was to organize it, rather than to say anything new. Even John of Damascus (d. 749) who wrote *On the Orthodox Faith* says little on the Ascension.

Those who wrote in Latin also looked to the past. The golden age of the Roman Empire was held in mind as the tribes from the north and east settled in the former Western Roman Empire. The focus of the monasteries was on devotion rather than doctrine, and even those writers who did bring fresh thought to doctrine passed over the Ascension.

Yet a few nuggets come to us from this period.

Bede (d. 735) in his Sermon on the Ascension says that the

Ascension was the ground of the Sacraments. He sees the parallels between Elijah and Christ. Elijah left his cloak, with which he had been clothed, to his disciple Elisha, so Christ left his disciples the Sacraments of the humanity which he had assumed to sanctify them.

Theophanis Ceramei (dates uncertain, but probably about 900), Archbishop of Taormina in Sicily, focuses on the cloud and sees in it a link to the role of the Holy Spirit in Jesus' incarnation.

> But the cloud was the Holy Spirit; for it is impossible for a perceptible cloud to pass beyond the upper air, where the moisture is naturally consumed by the heavenly fire. But as He descended by the Spirit, when Gabriel spoke thus to the Virgin: 'The Holy Ghost shall come upon thee', so He ascended accompanied by the Spirit. (Quoted in Davies, 1958, p 151)

Theophanis summarizes what Jesus has achieved in his 49th Homily: 'He deified the flesh by the union and offered immortality by the Resurrection and made us worthy of perfect reconciliation with the Father by the Ascension which He called the opening of heaven.'

Aelred (d. 1166), the English abbot of the Cistercian monastery at Rievaulx, saw Elijah's cloak, instead, as a pointer to the Church. 'When Elijah ascended in the chariot he left his cloak to Elisha, and when our Lord ascended into heaven, He commended His Church to His disciples' (quoted in Davies, 1958, p. 163).

Peter of Blois (d. 1211), a Breton priest who served for some of his life in England, argues that the Ascension proves the resurrection. 'For who would believe the Resurrection unless the Ascension had proved it? ... The flesh of Christ could not have ascended into heaven unless the virtue of the Resurrection had glorified it and rendered it immune and free from every burden of mortality' (Sermon 23).

What the First Theologians Wrote about the Ascension

Thomas Aquinas

Thomas Aquinas (d. 1247), an Italian Dominican friar, brought all his thoughts on theology together in one work, the *Summa Theologica*. Part 3, question 57 covers his views on the Ascension.

Aquinas defends the Ascension against those who say that, since Jesus was God, he could not be said to move and so could not ascend. He argues that Christ's body remained a creature and so could move, while his divinity does not. This means that,

> Although Christ's bodily presence was withdrawn from the faithful by the Ascension, still the presence of His Godhead is ever with the faithful, as He Himself says 'Behold, I am with you all days, even to the consummation of the world.' For, 'by ascending into heaven He did not abandon those whom He adopted,' as Pope Leo says (De Resurrec., Serm. ii). But Christ's Ascension into heaven, whereby He withdrew His bodily presence from us, was more profitable for us than His bodily presence would have been ... But when Christ withdrew in body, not only the Holy Ghost, but both Father and Son were present with them spiritually. (*Summa Theologica* 3.57.1)

In the 6th Article of this question, Aquinas defends the idea that the Ascension is necessary for our salvation:

> Christ's Ascension is the cause of our salvation in two ways: first of all, on our part; secondly, on His.
> On our part, in so far as by the Ascension our souls are uplifted to Him; because, as stated above (A[1], ad 3), His Ascension fosters, first, faith; secondly, hope; thirdly, charity. Fourthly, our reverence for Him is thereby increased, since we no longer deem Him an earthly man, but the God of heaven.
> On His part, in regard to those things which, in ascending, He did for our salvation. First, He prepared the way for our ascent into heaven, according to His own saying (John 14.2): 'I go to prepare a place for you,' Secondly, because as the

high-priest under the Old Testament entered the holy place to stand before God for the people, so also Christ entered heaven 'to make intercession for us,' as is said in Hebrews 7.25. Because the very showing of Himself in the human nature which He took with Him to heaven is a pleading for us ... so that for the very reason that God so exalted human nature in Christ, He may take pity on them for whom the Son of God took human nature. Thirdly, that being established in His heavenly seat as God and Lord, He might send down gifts upon men, according to Eph. 4.10: 'He ascended above all the heavens, that He might fill all things,' that is, 'with His gifts,' according to the gloss. (*Summa Theologica* 3.57.6)

Aquinas then discusses the item in the creed which says that Christ sits at the right hand of God the Father. This makes clear that the Ascension is about Jesus' humanity coming to heaven.

> Christ as man is exalted to Divine honour; and this is signified in the aforesaid sitting; nevertheless such honour belongs to Him as God, not through any assumption, but through His origin from eternity. (*Summa Theologica* 3.58.2)

Having said this of Christ's body when dealing with the Ascension, Aquinas goes on to speak of the bread and wine in Holy Communion as Jesus' body and blood. He says,

> This belongs to Christ's love, out of which for our salvation He assumed a true body of our nature. And because it is the special feature of friendship to live together with friends, as the Philosopher says (Ethic. Ix), He promises us His bodily presence as a reward. (*Summa Theologica* 3.75.1)

And then things go quiet. In the East the scholars and preachers hang on to the traditions they have received; in the West the scholars are content to rewrite and reorder what they have. It takes a major revolution in church life, the Reformation, to get people to think afresh about the Ascension.

10

The Reformation and the Enlightenment: Use and Dismissal of the Ascension

The Reformation

In the fifteenth century there were some significant discoveries. The boundaries of the known world were extended with the voyages to what is now America. A successful printing press with moveable type was invented by Gutenberg and made the copying of books possible on a larger scale. Erasmus published the New Testament in Greek, something that had not been seen in the West for many centuries.

There were abuses in the Church, including the selling of indulgences, and Martin Luther was so distressed by these that in 1517 he posted his ideas or 'theses' on the local notice board of the Wittenberg University, which was the church door. He and others sought to reform the Church, to remove the abuses, but had no intention of splitting it. Unfortunately, the senior members of the Church did not welcome reformation and the split came.

Over the next decades new thinking was needed to cope with this. If the Church is the place where Christ is met through Holy Communion and preaching, how do you know what is really the Church? What is the nature of Holy Communion in the new groups? Along with other doctrines, the Ascension was used to help find answers to these questions.

Martin Luther

Luther (d. 1546) wanted to reject the abuses of the Church, but not most of the things that it taught. When it came to Holy Communion, he pointed to the fact that Jesus said 'this is my body' at the Last Supper. Thus, the bread and wine as his body and blood is to be shown from Scripture and to be believed. When questioned about how this could be, since Jesus is at the right hand of the Father, he answered that while Jesus may have gone there, it did not mean that he was confined to heaven as a 'place in the sky'. Since he shares the divine omnipresence, he can be everywhere, including in the bread and wine (*The Sacrament of the Body and Blood – Against the Fanatics* Part 1).

John Calvin

Calvin (d. 1564) rejected Luther's idea of the Christ who is everywhere. He wanted to maintain the concreteness of the incarnation. So, for Calvin, if you wanted to know where Jesus was, the answer was heaven, a place beyond the whole machinery of the visible world.

In his commentary on Ephesians 4.10, Calvin says,

> 10. *That ascended up far above all heavens;* that is, beyond this created world. When Christ is said to be in heaven, we must not view him as dwelling among the spheres and numbering the stars. Heaven denotes a place higher than all the spheres, which was assigned to the Son of God after his resurrection. Not that it is literally a place beyond the world, but we cannot speak of the kingdom of God without using our ordinary language.

In the *Institutes of Religion* 4.17.30 he argues against those who say that Christ's body can be everywhere.

> Unless the body of Christ can be everywhere without any boundaries of space, it is impossible to believe that he is hid in

the Supper under the bread. Hence, they have been under the necessity of introducing the monstrous dogma of ubiquity. But it has been demonstrated by strong and clear passages of Scripture, first, that it is bounded by the dimensions of the human body; and, secondly, that its ascension into heaven made it plain that it is not in all places, but on passing to a new one, leaves the one formerly occupied.

In *Institutes of Religion* 4.17.27 he argued that the Ascension shows that Jesus body was moved to heaven and there his followers will go eventually.

Does not the very name of ascension, so often repeated, intimate removal from one place to another? This they deny, because by height, according to them, the majesty of empire only is denoted ... [He then refers to the words of the angels to the disciples.] By ascending to heaven, while you looked on, he has asserted his heavenly power: it remains for you to wait patiently until he again arrive to judge the world. He has not entered into heaven to occupy it alone, but to gather you and all the pious along with him.

So how does Christ who is in heaven relate now to his followers on earth? Calvin does not reject the presence of Christ in the sacrament despite his rejection of the ubiquity of Christ. The answer is that the Holy Spirit links us to Christ. So, earlier in section 17 of Book 4 of the *Institutes*, we read:

But though it seems an incredible thing that the flesh of Christ, while at such a distance from us in respect of place, should be food to us, let us remember how far the secret virtue of the Holy Spirit surpasses all our conceptions, and how foolish it is to wish to measure its immensity by our feeble capacity. Therefore, what our mind does not comprehend let faith conceive – viz. that the Spirit truly unites things separated by space.

Ulrich Zwingli

Zwingli (d. 1531) rejected the idea that Christ was in the bread and wine in any way in what he called the Lord's Supper, and it was to his ideas that Luther addressed his work *The Sacrament of the Body and Blood – Against the Fanatics*.

To argue against Luther, he pointed out that Christ is at the right hand of God. This is a contradiction with the idea that he is physically in the bread and wine: you cannot be bodily in two places at once. This argument is called the 'real absence'.

> A sacrament is the sign of a holy thing. When I say 'the sacrament of the Lord's body', I am simply referring to that bread which is the symbol of the body of Christ who was put to death for our sakes ... But the real body of Christ is the body which is seated at the right hand of God, and the sacrament of his body is the bread, and the sacrament of his blood is the wine, of which we partake with thanksgiving. Now the sign and the thing signified cannot be one and the same. Therefore the sacrament of the body of Christ cannot be that body itself. (*On the Lord's Supper*)

Zwingli does not tell us much about the Ascension but does show how those who are relying on Scripture alone can still disagree about something important in Christianity.

The Enlightenment and Romanticism

Beginning in the seventeenth century, the Enlightenment was, according to Immanuel Kant, 'Mankind's final coming of age, the emancipation of the human consciousness from an immature state of ignorance and error' (*Answering the Question: What is Enlightenment*, 1784). This freedom was gained by the use of reason, and by rejecting what could not be shown by reason. Allied to this use of reason was the growth of the scientific method. This is based on observation of the world and testing any conclusions to see if they really stand up. One outcome of this method was the realization that the Earth goes round the Sun, rather than the other way round. The view of the world with 'hell' below and 'heaven' above was seen not to be real. This challenged those who saw the Ascension as a literal event in which Jesus went up through the air to heaven.

One reaction to the rationalism of the Enlightenment was the Romanticism movement. This started in the second half of the eighteenth century and involved music and art as well as philosophy. Romanticism emphasized intuition and emotion against rationalism.

Such an environment led to a rethinking of the key events of Christianity and to a new phase of thought on the Ascension.

Friedrich Schleiermacher

As a young preacher at the Charite hospital in Berlin, Schleiermacher (d. 1834) shared rooms with Friedrich Schlegel, who taught him about the ideas of Romanticism.

Schleiermacher applied these ideas to his faith and argued that the area of feelings was the place for theological reflection. So, thinking about God starts with the believers' own consciousness and their experience of the community of the Church. This led to a radical appraisal of the resurrection and Ascension. They were to be seen not so much as about what happened to Jesus but rather as things that happen to us.

Schleiermacher as a Protestant was used to seeing preaching as the heart of a church service. But when he preached he was not seeking an intellectual response, but saw his words as bringing inner life. This was because he was preaching as part of the community of the Church, which itself derived from Jesus' giving of himself in teaching and in what he did. The Church re-enacts what it has received from Christ in its preaching and its sacraments. These form in people the Christian consciousness: they share the mind of Christ and are together his body on earth. So for Schleiermacher the Ascension of Christ is insignificant; what matters is his living presence in the Church, which is his earthly body.

Søren Kierkegaard

Kierkegaard (d. 1855) was a Danish philosopher and theologian who was interested in the question of how to really be a Christian. He rejected the idea that objective study of the Bible would achieve this, since he saw historical and critical searches for the truth at best leading only to something that is approximately the truth, and which did not lead to real happiness. What was needed was something subjective, something that dealt with our inner selves.

> [F]aith does not result from straightforward scholarly deliberation, nor does it come directly; on the contrary, in this objectivity one loses that infinite, personal, impassioned interestedness, which is the condition of faith, the *ubique et nusquam* [everywhere and nowhere] in which faith can come into existence. (Kierkegaard, 1992, p. 29)

Kierkegaard holds together Christ's humiliation and his exaltation. For Kierkegaard the doctrine of the Ascension says that they are one and the same. Jesus' Ascension was not to be seen as a triumphant new phase in the history of the world – *our* history. Rather, it is the way in which we can be sure that the crucified Christ is our contemporary. So, the presence of Jesus of Nazareth to us today is not through an intellectual assent to what he was 2000 years ago, nor some prolongation of his incarnation as such, but rather the fact that 'Jesus-history' is absolute and our history is relative to it. Jesus, who ascended and will come, puts himself as a question to each of us and our history is being judged by his. He is absolute; the rest of what we see can only be judged in relation to him. We each face the question, 'What shall I do with this Jesus who is called the Christ?'

For Kierkegaard Christianity was not about bringing humans together, but for each of them to stand separately before God. Only when truly united with God would they be united to others.

D. F. Strauss

The response of Strauss (d. 1874) to the Enlightenment was to reject the Ascension as a physical elevation into the air. He did not want to go as far as others who tried to remove all miraculous elements from the Gospels, and so developed the use of the word 'myth' to mean a theological idea expressed in a narrative. He argued that the narrative about the Ascension was never meant to be taken literally, but was a story told to show the early Church's belief that Jesus was exalted with God. He saw the story as having drawn on the Old Testament picture of the Son of Man coming on the clouds of heaven to God.

Hans Martensen

Martensen (d. 1884) was a Danish Lutheran bishop who in his *Christian Dogmatics*, published in 1874, aimed to interpret Lutheran traditions in a way that suited modern reason. For him, in Jesus there was a descending of the divine and an ascending of the creaturely. Through Jesus' resurrection a new way of being was available for the world, where the 'energies of the future' are available now (Martensen, 1874, p. 318). The Ascension is the 'close of the resurrection and the perfecting expression and act of exaltation' (Martensen, 1874, p. 320). But we should not think that Jesus is in some particular place – heaven is everywhere God is. But now that he is lifted up Jesus is able to show his perfect union with the Father, and 'when he is lifted up above the limits of time and space, then for the first time He was able to unfold and display His organic relations to the children of men, by the all-attractive power of His Spirit and His Word' (Martensen, 1874, p. 322). So, for Martensen, the important thing in the Ascension is Jesus being taken out of the limitations of our human existence, and the coming of the Spirit that brings him to us and us to him.

At each stage in the 400 years we have just surveyed the authors were writing to deal with the ideas circulating at the time. At the Reformation they were dealing with how to be the Church now that the Church was divided. At the Enlightenment they were dealing with how to understand the Bible and Christian tradition when a scientific view of the world was unfolding. Each dealt with this in a different way, emphasizing one aspect of what they had received over another, until they were content with how their faith was expressed in their time. As we move to look at the twentieth century the ideas and challenges change fast.

11

The Ascension in the Twentieth Century: The Recovery of the Doctrine

In the twentieth century Christians continued to wrestle with the idea of the Ascension against the backdrop of an increasingly scientific understanding of the world. They also had to deal with the emotional impact of two world wars.

The earlier twentieth century

Adolf von Harnack

Von Harnack[1] (d. 1930) was a German Lutheran theologian who followed Strauss's idea of the Ascension as a 'myth' which expressed Jesus' exaltation. It was a legend that developed slowly over the years after Jesus' resurrection, and he saw three stages in the development of the narrative:

(1) The Ascension in the oldest preaching, such as 1 Corinthians 15, Matthew 28 and Mark 16.1–8, was not separated from the resurrection and exaltation, which were one idea.
(2) In his Gospel, Luke added Luke 9.51, 'When the days drew near for him to be taken up, he set his face to go to Jerusalem.' He also added the story at Luke 24.50–53 even though he knew it wasn't literally true.

---

[1] Unless otherwise referenced, this chapter relies on the excellent survey of work on the Ascension in A. W. Zweip, 1997, *The Ascension of the Messiah in Lukan Christology*, Supplements to Novum Testamentum, vol. 87.

(3) Finally, when Acts was written the author added the detailed narrative with the Ascension story set 40 days later on the Mount of Olives, deliberately recalling the narrative of Elijah's assumption.

Others, such as Eduard Meyer (1855–1930), suggested that Luke 24.50–53 was original to Luke, but Acts 1.2–14 was a second-century addition by someone who was a gnostic (that is, who believed that the special people could rise to know God as he really is through being taught secret knowledge). The addition of the '40 days' was to give Jesus time to impart his secret teaching to the apostles.

V. Larranaga, in his *Thesis on the Ascension* (1938), decided that Acts 1.2–14 was part of the original text since the vocabulary and ways of writing matched the rest of Acts so well. He also argued that Harnack himself put Acts as written in AD 58–62 and so there wasn't time for the slow development of a legend.

The French Roman Catholic priest Pierre Benoit, in his 1949 work *L'Ascension*, argued that the longer time before the Ascension was in fact necessary for the disciples to be convinced of the resurrection. He suggested that there were two different theological ideas which were both called the 'Ascension' but actually distinct. The first was the invisible exaltation to God's right hand that occurred at, or soon after, the resurrection. This was followed by Jesus' appearances, which came to an end with the visible Ascension after 40 days. This second occurred because humans needed to see that Jesus had gone to God and been exalted, and is secondary to the first. This is why the New Testament authors so often mentioned Jesus' exaltation without referring to the Ascension.

Rudolf Bultmann

Bultmann (d. 1976), the German Lutheran Professor of New Testament at the University of Marburg, resolved the problems of the historicity of the resurrection and the Ascension by dismissing both as historical events. What was important was faith in Jesus as Christ; how he came to be so was secondary. Bultmann had a programme of 'demythologizing' the Bible, analysing the text to distinguish the original facts from what had been added by the early Christian authors. For Bultmann what had been added was fascinating – what was it about Jesus that led his followers to invent stories about his birth and life to express what he had meant to them? Bultmann concluded that Jesus did not see himself as the Son of God or Son of Man. What mattered for faith was the impact of his death on the individual, hence the dismissal of the Ascension as a valueless story.

David Edwards (Edwards, 1976, p. 728) says that Bultmann's theology is best seen in 'his little book of lectures to young Americans in 1951, *Jesus Christ and Mythology* (Scribner's, 1958). All his thoughts were unified around the desire of his heart to encourage or to shock students of theology into preaching a relevant Christ.'

The historical background to Bultmann's work is the two world wars. In the second he prepared the chaplains to the German army for the experiences they would face. He saw in Christ's cross the place for faith to be born.

> On the wood of the cross, the existence of this strange man was questioned by the hard nails of the world. In every generation those who decided for themselves that the crucified Jesus was right – rather than his enemies – had Christian faith, and the rising of their faith was the one perpetual miracle. It was the Easter of faith in a world naturally progressing toward winter. (Edwards, 1976, p. 728)

Michael Ramsey

Ramsey, who was Archbishop of Canterbury from 1961 to 1974, concluded in his article 'What was the Ascension?' (Ramsey, 1951) that,

> No man saw the resurrection happen, and no man saw the ascension happen either. The story in Acts 1, even taken very literally, does not tell us that men saw Jesus leave earth or

enter heaven. But we have ... some evidence that the disciples were granted a vision which brought home to them not only the resurrection but also the glorious heavenly status of their Master. What is precarious is Luke's placing of this event in the scheme of his history.

For Ramsey, Jesus ascended as the ending of the journey that was his whole earthly life, a journey to the Father. This is Jesus' glorification and 'it seems right to infer that before Jesus comes and breathes the Holy Spirit upon the church on the evening of Easter Day the Ascension had clearly happened'. What happened in Acts 1 was a 'theophany', that is, the revelation of God, which marks the turning point from the time that Jesus was seen to the time when he is the invisible Lord.

Karl Barth

Barth (d. 1968) was a Swiss Reformed theologian. The heart of his theology is that we can know nothing about God unless he chooses to reveal it to us. So all our work is to reflect on what God has shown us. The key revelation of himself is in the coming of the Word, that is, Jesus.

Barth dismisses the idea that we can bring our fallen reason to Jesus and judge him by it. Rather, all our thoughts must be judged by the reality that is Jesus, his life, death and glorification, as the deepest revelation of who God is. Thus, he rejects the 'demythologizing tendency' of some of the German theologians.

While few pages are given in Barth's works directly to the Ascension, he uses it at significant points. The Ascension means that Jesus is physically absent from earth, but that he will come again. The Church is to live with this reality each day – Jesus being absent but expected.

Barth, like others, is not interested in seeing the Ascension in terms of movement; rather, the risen Jesus with his humanity goes to the Father's side and enters the hiddenness of God. For Barth the Ascension is a real event, and one with meaning: 'both the empty tomb and the ascension are merely signs of the Easter event ... Yet both are so important that we can hardly say that they might equally well be omitted' (*Church Dogmatics* III/2, p. 453).

The Easter event is what leads Jesus to be the Lord of heaven and earth, both beyond the universe (transcendent) and active within it now. But how can he be both transcendent yet active here? The answer for Barth is that Jesus is absent in his physical humanity, but the Church is the 'earthly historical form of Jesus' continued existence, the place where the Spirit creates knowledge of God and genuine human response to Jesus as God's word' (Burgess, 2004, p. 189). This does not mean that the Church takes on the role of Jesus' humanity – that is ascended and 'located' at the Father's right hand in heaven. But the Church is Jesus' body, an earthly expression within history of his activity, and is his body only in union with its heavenly Head who is ascended with his human body to the Father. It is not Jesus' primary body, but is derived from Jesus' humanity and divinity, a place where the Holy Spirit is active and witnessing to Jesus. Thus, the Church is not perfect, it is not Jesus' humanity as such; rather, Christians live in the 'time between' the Ascension and the return of Jesus, and are still sinners though they will be seen to be redeemed when Jesus returns.

For Barth Jesus is ascended bodily. His being and his work as Saviour are veiled from us, but it is the ultimate reality of the time we live in. Jesus is Lord, active in the world by the Holy Spirit who is Jesus' witness to himself. As Burgess (2004, p. 201) says,

> Failure to attend to Jesus' ascension and ministry may allow theology to lose sight of the particular character of the age and of the mission and the task of both church and Christian within it. Mission may be lost in favour of maintenance of the church itself and the church and its life may come to be seen as an end in itself. Similarly, the world of the Christian may be lost in favour of an ethic of divine contemplation, or alternatively, the coming kingdom – held with Christ in heaven – may be reduced to an outcome of the processes of this age and

therefore the attempt may be made to bring it about within fallen history. (2004, p. 201)

J. G. Davies

Davies' magisterial work on the Ascension, published in 1958, underpinned much of what has been said in Chapter 9 on the Ascension in church history before the Reformation. He gave the Bampton Lectures in the University of Oxford in 1958 on the theme of the Ascension since, 'Of all the articles in the Creed there is none that has been so neglected in the present century as that which affirms our Lord's Ascension into heaven' (Davies, 1958, p. 9).

He sees the cause of the neglect as the increased scientific awareness of the nineteenth century. The Ascension narratives, which presumed a view of the world with a flat earth, hell below, and heaven above to be risen into, were embarrassing and best ignored. So, as we have seen, Harnack developed his view of the Ascension as a theological story which did not actually happen, and most thinkers followed his lead.

Davies then reviewed what the Bible had to say on the Ascension and found every reference to it in the works of theology of the first 14 centuries. He concludes that there is much more to be said about the Ascension than can be developed from the narrative of Acts 1 alone. Indeed, if Acts 1 is made the focus people will tend to see the Ascension as more to do with the end of the resurrection appearances than anything else. Davies dismisses Luke's account in Acts as historically unreliable but sees it as containing important theological ideas.

> We need not then believe that the Ascension involved transportation to a localized heaven but transference to a new condition of being which, in the felicitous words of an early eighteenth-century writer on the subject, 'far better becometh the Divine Residence than the Top of our Atmosphere.' (Davies, 1958, p. 14)

The Ascension in the Twentieth Century

Davies sees the Ascension as a real event but one that occurred on Easter Day, closely linked to the resurrection. 'It consummates the reconciliation between man and God which is effected by God putting Himself in man's place at the Incarnation and by man being put in God's place at the Ascension' (Davies, 1958, p. 169). In the resurrection, where death was conquered, Christ's humanity was transformed so as to not be mortal; in the Ascension that transformed humanity entered a new way of existing in heaven. In heaven Jesus' humanity enters the Temple of God, heaven itself, and is offered as the first fruits of humanity, making all humanity holy. He is the ascended Head of the Church, and

> [h]is Body glorified through Resurrection and Ascension, is now the centre and substance of His mystical Body, the Church – hence the virtual identity between them. But since 'it is not yet made manifest what we shall be' [1 John 3.2], since, that is to say, our present condition is in contrast with His present condition, the two must be distinguished in our understanding. We have received the pledge but not the fullness of our inheritance. (Davies, 1958, p. 173)

Davies points to the one New Testament passage that gives a reason for the Ascension. In Ephesians 4.10 Christ ascended 'that he might fill all things'. Davies sees this as Christ filling the universe with his divine activity as 'Sovereign and Governor, thereby claiming it as His rightful possession' (Davies, 1958, p. 177).

Faith unites us now with the ascended Lord, and the Ascension gives us a firm hope that we will be where he is now. In the meantime Christ is with us, by the sacrament of Holy Communion and by the word. Now we reflect his glory because his Spirit is working in us, but we will at the end of all things be changed into glory and will see him as he really is.

The Missing Ending

Hans Conzelmann

Conzelmann (d. 1989) was a German theologian who was severely wounded in the Second World War. He suggested that Luke's account of the Ascension was written to show that the delay of Jesus' second coming was part of God's plans. His followers may have expected him to return soon, but actually Jesus was saying that his return would be sudden rather than soon. So there are three periods of history:

(a) The time of Israel until the coming of John the Baptist;
(b) the time of Jesus from the coming of John the Baptist to the Ascension;
(c) the time of the Church from the Ascension until Jesus' return.

Thus, the Ascension is the beginning of the period of the Church.

P. A. Van Stempvoort

Van Stempvoort reminds his readers in his article 'The Interpretation of the Ascension in Luke and Acts', written in 1958, that the Church did not fix the celebration of the Ascension as the fortieth day after Easter until the fourth century.

Van Stempvoort looks at the detail of Luke 24.50–53 and notes that Jesus leads his disciples out of Jerusalem. He sees this as linking back to the events before the crucifixion, when Jesus' way led over the Mount of Olives *into* Jerusalem. Now he starts his disciples on their journey *away* from Jerusalem towards the ends of the earth.

Luke does not give any particular time pointers in this version of his story. He is not aiming to set this story in history as such. Here Jesus commissions his disciples with his priestly blessing; Van Stempvoort notes that the term 'lifting up his hands' is the technical term for the priest preparing to give the blessing. He sees Luke deliberately drawing on passages such as Sirach 50.20–21:

> Then Simon came down and raised his hands
> over the whole congregation of Israelites,
> to pronounce the blessing of the Lord with his lips,
> and to glory in his name;
> and they bowed down in worship a second time,
> to receive the blessing from the Most High.

Here the priest blesses the people and their response is to fall down in worship (*proskynesantes*). Just so in Luke 24:

> Then he led them out as far as Bethany, and, lifting up his hands, he blessed them. While he was blessing them, he withdrew from them and was carried up into heaven. And they worshipped (*proskynesantes*) him, and returned to Jerusalem with great joy; and they were continually in the temple blessing God. (Luke 24.50–53)

Van Stempvoort argues that Luke is deliberately ending his Gospel with a priestly blessing and the Church in worship of the blessing, ascending Christ. However, he does not leave the Church there. He starts his second book by dealing with the Ascension again.

When discussing Acts, Van Stempvoort sees Luke now using clear time and geographical pointers to emphasize the reality of the Ascension in history, and as a pointer forward. He notes that many translations of what the cloud did make it mystical – 'the cloud hid him' – but the simplest, most basic translation of the word *ypolamb* is 'to get under', 'to carry'. So Luke sees the cloud as lifting Jesus up – it is his way of leaving – on the cloud. The disciples strain to see him and the angels affirm that he is physically gone for good this time. So the Ascension story this time is pointing to the future, both to Jesus' eventual return, but also to the immediate future, to be worked out in the Church, by the power of the Holy Spirit.

The later twentieth century and beyond

Eric Franklin

Franklin wrote his article 'The Ascension and Eschatology of Acts' in 1970. He argues that, for Luke, what God will do in the last days, God's ultimate action, is focused not on Jesus' future return but on the Ascension.

For Luke the Ascension, which concludes his Gospel, is the viewpoint to understand Jesus' life. The way to Jerusalem is the way to his departure, his Ascension, with all that he has accomplished there. So when Stephen sees a vision of heaven, he sees Jesus' exaltation. Revelation of Jesus' glory does not wait for Jesus' return; through the Ascension it is a reality now.

By putting the Ascension at the start of Acts, Luke makes clear that 'history since the ascension is about witnessing to it as the moment of the enthronement of Jesus at the right hand of God' (Franklin, 1970, p. 194). Jesus has his full authority now, not at some distant future time – *now* he is both Lord and Christ. 'Salvation is guaranteed, not by belief in a past event [i.e., the crucifixion] but by responding to the present Lordship of Jesus (Acts 3.26, 5.31, 17.31, 26.23)' (Franklin, 1970, p. 195). The gift of the Spirit and the mission of the Church are derived from the Ascension; they are the result of it on earth, and they give its effect in people's lives. But Franklin does not see the Holy Spirit as bringing Jesus to people but as enabling them to witness to Jesus. To reject this witness is to reject the Holy Spirit, and so is unforgivable.

Jesus is in his kingdom, it exists now, but on earth it can only be seen by those with faith. It can come to believers as they take communion, which is a foretaste of the banquet of heaven, and Jesus' followers live as those who are under Jesus' kingship. So Jesus' kingship in heaven breaks through to the earth now. As the witness to Jesus is taken as far as Rome, this is seen as the guarantee that what happened in Jerusalem was the ultimate event, which God had done in the world, through Jesus. It is the Ascension, not the looked-for return of Jesus, which is the climax of history.

G. Lohfink

Lohfink, in *Die Himmelfahrt Jesu* (1971), looked at Greco-Roman literature and the ascensions depicted there. He was analysing the 'form' of the stories, and this is called 'form criticism'. He found two varieties, the heavenly journey of the soul and the rapture, where the character is taken physically into heaven. In the first type of story the upward journey is the key, rather than the arrival at the goal, while in the second where the character goes from and to are important: they go from the human world to the gods. In such stories the viewpoint is that of those left on earth, with witnesses playing a vital role. The typical themes or motifs of these stories are mountains, fire, lightning, storms, chariots, eagles and clouds. There are often other phenomena which accompany the rapture, such as an eclipse, earthquakes, some sort for confirmation from heaven, and subsequent veneration of the one who has gone.

The Old Testament Apocrypha had two further versions of ascension: that of the soul at death, while the body remains in the grave, and the ascent of an angel at the end of an appearance. Other heavenly journeys in Jewish literature consist of a revelation given to a person who goes to heaven and returns. A Jewish tale will always involve the person's body as well as their soul being caught up to heaven.

Lohfink concludes that, in Acts, Luke used the typical themes of a rapture story – the Ascension occurs up a mountain, with cloud and subsequent worship, so its 'form' is that of a Greco-Roman rapture story. The narrative is recorded from the point of view of the human witness and there is heavenly confirmation from the angels. In Luke the story focuses on Jesus' blessing and the disciples' worship of Jesus. Each account fits its purpose so well that Lohfink sees them both as created by Luke for his theological purpose. He took the early tradition of Jesus being exalted and produced stories to say how this happened, not to give literal history but to express his views of Jesus.

The Missing Ending

C. H. Talbert

Talbert in 1974 looked at the accounts in Luke and Acts to see how they fitted into the style of writing of the first century AD. He sees the author of these works as a consummate artist. Luke is not just writing to record facts but to build a picture for the reader.

Talbert proposes something which he calls Architectural Analysis. He looks for patterns in the overall structure of the work and compares it with similar patterns in other works, thus highlighting the cultural or aesthetic roots of the way Luke writes. As he says:

> It is not possible to speak of a unique Christian aesthetic at this early stage of the Christian community's life. Early Christianity was part of the general Mediterranean culture of the time which, by virtue of both its classical and Near Eastern roots, was characterised by a strong predisposition to balance in all types of self-expression. Early Christianity shared this predisposition and we have seen it come to light in both literature and art. (Talbert, 1974, p. 77)

So Talbert looked for balance but did not expect it to be perfect since slight asymmetry was the ideal in classical literature.

Talbert argues that Luke used this style technique to help his readers remember what he has written and as a result see the overall pattern of who Jesus is. His readers would also be attuned to how they have heard of Jesus before and so would be aware of what emphases Luke is giving by his changes from his sources.

Applying this to Luke's accounts of the Ascension, Talbert argues that the Ascension is critical for Luke's understanding of his work. Greco-Roman and Jewish writers both had their key point at the centre of their work. Luke-Acts fits this. From Luke 9.51 the Gospel moves towards the Ascension. In Acts 'everything moves out from the Ascension'.

Luke in Acts distinguishes the Ascension from the resurrection-exaltation – Talbert argues that Paul did not know of an ascension separate from the resurrection and exaltation of Jesus. The reason Luke emphasizes the Ascension is that for him it acts as a guarantee. It guarantees the corporeality (bodiliness) of the one who ascends, since the Ascension is portrayed as an observable event. Luke has emphasized Jesus' bodiliness in his description of Jesus' sufferings (e.g., 'They did not find the body', Luke 24.22). Talbert suggests that Luke was responding to a tendency by some of his contemporaries to see the Ascension as purely spiritual.

The architecture of Luke's Gospel places the death and resurrection of Jesus in an 'Ascension framework'. In Luke 24.26 Jesus explains that his suffering was necessary for his entering into glory. The Ascension is not an escape from human miseries; it is through death that Jesus came to his Ascension and his glory.

Joseph A. Fitzmeyer

Fitzmeyer, an American Jesuit scholar, in his 1984 paper asks if Luke did indeed invent the Ascension. As he looks at the New Testament, he sees the earliest writing speaking of Christ's exaltation, but without saying how Jesus was taken up to the Father's presence. He points to Philippians 3.8–11 and 1 Timothy 3.16 as early fragments in later works, which refer to Jesus' exaltation. He also sees John's Gospel recording this tradition. He then notes that within Acts the snippets of preaching that have a summary of the basis of faith (these are called the *kerygma* by scholars) link Jesus' exaltation to his resurrection.

Other passages in the New Testament do describe the Ascension, particularly Luke 24.50–53, where the Ascension occurs on Easter Sunday, and in Acts where it occurs 40 days later. In the Acts passage, Fitzmeyer comments that 'Luke has employed apocalyptic stage-props to recount the ascension of Christ' (Fitzmeyer, 1984, p. 419).

To resolve the difficulty of the timing of the Ascension Fitzmeyer reminds us that Jesus' resurrection was not a resuscitation – he did not return exactly as he was before. He also points out that the appearance accounts don't tell us where he has come from. He comes and goes, but where does he go to? In Luke 24.26, Jesus says to his followers, 'Was it not necessary that the Messiah should suffer these things and then enter into his glory?' Jesus implies that he has already entered his glory, which is the glory of the Father's presence. So when Jesus appears to his disciples he is coming to them from his Father's glory – that is, coming from heaven. Fitzmeyer concludes that 'his ascension is nothing more than the appearance from glory in which Christ took his final leave from the community of his followers – his last visible leave taking from his assembled followers' (Fitzmeyer, 1984, p. 424).

Fitzmeyer summarizes, 'Luke has not invented the "ascension" as something distinct from Jesus' resurrection – that was in the tradition before him – but he has *historicized* it in a way that no other NT writer has, by his introduction of the "forty days".' Still it acts as 'the guarantee of Christian destiny' (Fitzmeyer, 1984, p. 425).

T. F. Torrance

The Scottish presbyterian scholar T. F. Torrance's work *Space, Time and Resurrection* was first published in 1976. Although much of the book is about the resurrection, Torrance also looks at the Ascension.

Torrance rejects Barth's idea that our reason is completely flawed. Rather, '[God] is actively at work in the world in revealing himself in cognitive ways to those whom he has made for communion with himself' (Torrance, 1998, p. 2). However, he also rejects the idea that Christian doctrines are built up by taking what the Bible says as logical propositions, with us as observers who deduce the truth from our observational data. Rather, we are involved, not impartial, observers of what God has done.

For Torrance 'It is with the ascension that Jesus Christ was fully installed in his kingly ministry' (Torrance, 1976, p. 106). Jesus was born to be king, and was crowned with thorns, but when he was exalted to the throne of God his reign began in earnest. He brought with him his vocation as a prophet which he had exercised in his teaching ministry, and he acted as a priest by offering himself in sacrifice, both in his death and in his resurrection, which is offered in eternity to God the Father. He is also priestly in his ongoing advocacy for humanity. He as human and divine offers the prayer and worship which humanity otherwise could not offer. But Jesus' priesthood does not just look to God; rather, 'Pentecost is the content and the actualization of that high priestly blessing' (Torrance, 1976, p. 116).

Because Jesus is the High Priest, the Church is a royal priesthood, each Christian participating in the one priesthood of Christ through our service of him. Torrance says that the New Testament does not speak of a 'priesthood of all believers', for it no more speaks of the individual as a 'priest' than it does of him as a 'king'. 'The priesthood of the church is not constituted of the aggregation of the priestly functions of its individual members but is only a reflection of the one individual priesthood of Christ' (Torrance, 1976, p. 118).

Torrance's work particularly explores how the resurrection and Ascension of Jesus relate to space and time as we experience them. So he says of Jesus, 'He really and fully became man, as we men are in space and time, and yet remained God the Creator who transcends all creaturely being in space and time' (Torrance, 1976, p. 126). When Jesus ascended it was 'an ascension beyond our notions of space and time' (Torrance, 1976, p. 127). When Christ ascended above all space and time he did not cease to be human, and there was no diminishment of his physical, historical existence. Just as the man Jesus 'is the place in this physical world of space and time where God and man meet and where they have communion with one another' (Torrance, 1976, p. 128), so the Church on earth, in the continuing space–time of this world, is the 'place' where God and humanity meet in humanity's place. In the incarnation, Man and God meet in Man's 'place', in the Ascension Man and God meet in God's 'place', and by the Spirit these two are not separated.

So, 'the ascension means that we cannot know God by transcending space and time, by leaping beyond the limits of our place on earth, but only by encountering God and his saving work within space and time, within our actual physical existence' (Torrance, 1976, p. 132). In the historical and crucified Jesus we meet with the risen and ascended Lord, through the Spirit. 'Through the Spirit Christ is nearer to us than we are to ourselves, and we who live and dwell on earth are yet made to sit with Christ "in the heavenly places", partaking of the divine nature with him' (Torrance, 1976, p. 135).

M. C. Parsons

Parsons published his PhD thesis in 1987 as *The Departure of Jesus in Luke-Acts*. In his work he first looks at the ways in which people try to unpick the text to find previous traditions which the author knew, as well as trying to find out what he has added and why. Such techniques are called together 'high criticism' and involve studying how the author has edited what he received (redaction analysis) or how he has presented it (narrative analysis) and what styles he has copied from elsewhere (form criticism), as well as seeking the underlying sources for what he has written (source criticism). Using these techniques Parsons sees the history of the traditions about the Ascension as being in three phases:

(1) Some texts place the Ascension on Easter Sunday, e.g., Mark 16.19, Barnabas 15.9.
(2) The Ascension is separated from the resurrection by a short period of time, about 40 or 50 days. Luke is the one who pinned it down as 40 days.
(3) Later texts from the gnostic writers had a longer gap still: for example, the Ascension of Isaiah 9.16 has 545 days, and in Pistis Sophia Jesus does not ascend until 12 years after the resurrection.

Parsons then looks at the two narratives of the Ascension as they are in the Bible. He answers the question as to why they differ, by saying that they had different *literary* functions in their respective books. Luke 24 is an ending to that book and

The Ascension in the Twentieth Century

Acts 1 is a beginning to Acts. It is their context that explains the differences in the details of the two narratives.

Luke 24.50–53	Acts 1.2–11	Reason for the difference
No new timing; information implies that the Ascension is on Easter Day	Refers to 40 days	In Luke the narrative is acting as an epilogue. The exaltation of Jesus is linked to his resurrection theologically so no gap of time is mentioned. In Acts the 40 days show that there was time for the disciples to be instructed by Jesus before his departure.
Place is Bethany, which links back to the triumphant entry to Jerusalem	Place is Mount of Olives, where Jesus often went to pray	In Luke the circle is made to Bethany, from where they went into Jerusalem. The triumphant entry is brought to its fulfilment in Jesus' exaltation. In Acts the link is to Jesus praying: the disciples return from the Mount to pray.
They return to the Temple to worship	They return to the upper room to pray	In Luke the Temple is mentioned; this is a closure device. They return to where Jesus had confronted the Temple authorities, but now he is exalted and vindicated. In Acts they return to be prepared for the next stage of the journey.

Luke 24.50–53	Acts 1.2–11	Reason for the difference
The disciples say nothing	The disciples have a dialogue with Jesus	In Luke the disciples are silent; this is a literary device which starts to make space between the reader and the story, and so enables it to end. In Acts the dialogue points forward to what is to come in the book.
Jesus blesses the disciples	Jesus is taken up on a cloud, and angels appear	Jesus blesses his disciples; this is a closing scene. In Acts the disciples are being commissioned for their task.

So, the passage in Luke has been moulded to act as an ending, with its motif of blessing, whereas the passage in Acts is beginning the book and setting the scene for what is to come next.

Rowan Williams

Rowan Williams is a former Archbishop of Canterbury as well as a scholar of early Church doctrines. For Williams, Jesus is not an idea but a living person. But since he is ascended we don't meet him directly, but rather through the people he has touched, and who have been equipped by him to 'take responsibility for his tangible presence in the world' (Williams, 2007, p. 93).

He sees the Ascension as the moment when Jesus 'goes away', stops being an object we concentrate on in itself and yet becomes deeply and more permanently present: 'I am with you always, to the end of time.' He is with us 'as the light we see by; we see the world in a new way because we see *through* him, see it with his eyes' (Williams, 1994, p. 82).

It means that we think about Jesus not as someone completely outside us, but as the power in us gradually setting us free to see the world with clarity, hope and love. Jesus does not greedily demand attention for himself: he points us to the God he calls Father and enables us to go on our journey towards God the Father as he himself did, by the path of commitment to the world. (Williams, 1994, p. 83)

A. Zweip

Zweip (1997), having reviewed other authors' ideas, concluded that the ascension narratives are at key points in the Luke-Acts work. The event is used to structure the work. In Luke it is pointed towards by Luke 9.51, and all the events from Luke 9 are leading towards the Ascension. Luke distinguishes Jesus' resurrection and exaltation from his Ascension: the post-resurrection appearances are those of an already exalted Lord, who comes from heaven.

In Acts the Ascension is the advance notice of the end of the world. The Ascension is told to help those who expected Jesus to return soon. Since his return is clearly delayed, they need to be reassured that it will happen: hence this story, with its promise of Jesus' return 'in like manner'.

R. Strelan

Strelan (2004) sets the Acts of the Apostles in the context of first-century culture. In the Greco-Roman world, the divine and the natural were seen as completely interlinked. An event could be given a natural explanation and a divine one at the same time. There is also a keen sense of 'paradoxia', things that could not be understood and so were seen as miracles. To show that there was only one God it was important to show his power and status through his acts. So, what may seem 'strange acts' to us are an important part of the communication of God in that culture. The signs and wonders of Acts serve to legitimate the mission to the Gentiles and to show that the Christian movement was of God. As Strelan says, 'Luke sees the heroes of his god as being in a turf war ... in Luke's story other sources of power and revelation are forced to concede to the greater dynamis [power] of his god and to the men empowered by that god' (Strelan, 2004, p. 29).

In this context, 'Jesus' ascension certainly does not mark his removal from any interest or involvement in the affairs of those whom he has commissioned to be witnesses, nor does it mark his absence from them' (Strelan, 2004, p. 40). For Luke there is no gulf between heaven and earth, so the Jesus who is exalted in heaven is active in the world of Acts.

M. Sleeman

M. Sleeman (2009) has a background in geography and sought to apply his insights from that discipline to the study of the Ascension. He aimed to show how Jesus' Ascension structures the Church in Acts and shapes the believers' 'spatiality'. There is a debate among those who study the Ascension about how to resolve the tension between Christ's absence and presence: is he inactive today in the world or active in some way?

To help resolve this tension, Sleeman turns to the tools of geography. Places come with meaning attached, as can be seen from the stereotypes of a declaration of love by moonlight on a balcony, a rendezvous at an inn and brawls in bars. So Sleeman introduces the concept, which the geographer Edward Soja pioneered, of 'thirdspace'. This is distinguished from 'firstspace', which is the physical, mappable ground, and 'secondspace', which is the way we describe that space mentally, as seen in an architectural plan or a written description. 'Thirdspace' brings the associations of the place together with its reality. Sleeman illustrates 'thirdspace' with three examples.

First, Rosa Parks got on a bus in Alabama in 1955 and sat down. When a white passenger got on, she refused to give up her space. This was a symbolic action which sparked a boycott of the buses. Where she was on the bus, the space she occupied, was not just a physical reality, but it had meaning. This meaning is the stuff of 'thirdspace'.

Second, in 1914 on the Western Front the space between the

trenches of the Germans and the British was No Man's Land. They fought over it fiercely, and no one could safely stay there. But on Christmas Day, an unofficial truce occurred in places, where the soldiers came out of their trenches, sang carols and even played football. They made 'No Man's Land' into 'Every Man's Land' for a day before returning to try to slaughter one another. So for a day the 'thirdspace' of that tract of land had different associations: they changed its 'thirdspace'.

Third, platform 9¾ at King's Cross Station is described in J. K. Rowling's books in the Harry Potter series. This is 'secondspace', a description of a place that may not be a real place in this world but can be described. In fact, there is now a feature at King's Cross station that is 'platform 9¾' – 'secondspace' has influenced 'firstspace'. But in the books, 'platform 9¾' is not just used as a physical place: rather, as the interface between the 'muggle' and the magical worlds it has a meaning in the books, and so has a 'thirdspace'.

Sleeman argues that if you read the narrative of Acts with this idea in mind you find an 'absent-but-active ascended Christ functioning thirdspatially within the narrative' (Sleeman, 2009, p. 44). So the Ascension is not just about departure, but about how Christ is active in the rest of Acts. The Ascension governs how the characters and the places develop in the book. 'But you will receive power when the Holy Spirit has come upon you; and you will be my witnesses in Jerusalem, in all Judea and Samaria, and to the ends of the earth' (Acts 1.8), is not just descriptive but a 'divine bird's-eye view of the world'.

Looking at the places referred to in the prologue to Acts, it assumes spaces (and their meanings) from Luke and anticipates the Ascension account which is about to be given. The disciples ask Jesus, 'Lord, is this the time when you will restore the kingdom to Israel?' (Acts 1.6)

This has three spatial assumptions:

(a) The restoration of the kingdom is to Israel, the country, with all its meaning as the place where God's chosen people live.
(b) Jesus is the one who *can* restore the kingdom. The promise

of Acts 1.11 looks to the time when this will happen in this place, but first his disciples are to be his witnesses in his 'firstspace' absence.
(c) Acts 1.6 presupposes that the restoration could happen now; the disciples see Jesus as powerful.

Jesus' response to their question (Acts 1.7–8) is to expand their horizons. He gets them to change their viewpoint from the singular Israel to a string of locations, to Jerusalem, all Judea and Samaria, and to the ends of the earth. These are not just physical geographical descriptors; Samaria comes with all the weight of the Jewish–Samaritan tensions of the last half millennium. So, the 'witness-space' is to breach the ethnic divides that defined 'Israel-space' and to go to the 'ends of the earth'. Again, this is not a specific location, but has the ring of God's ultimate action, the 'eschaton', seen not as the last days, but as the last places.

But Jesus' response to Acts 1.6 does not stop at verse 8. By his Ascension in verse 9 he gives a new 'thirdspace' to his disciples' destinations, they are all to be seen in relation to Christ in heaven. 'That Jesus is no longer physically present on earth means that they become necessary witnesses. There is no means by which to access Jesus other than through their testimony. Even the Spirit, from Acts 2 onwards, will be a presence which discloses absence' (Sleeman, 2009, p. 76). Every time heaven is mentioned after this in Acts, it will remind the hearer of Acts 1.6–11, with Jesus who has gone into heaven. So Jesus' response to the question in Acts 1.6 is far more than a yes or no answer: it is a new framework for all that will come.

By his Ascension Jesus becomes absent but active. By the commissioning of the disciples and the coming of the Spirit 'believer space' is formed. This is vital since, 'Apart from the possible exception of 8.39 (and if so 8.39 is exceptional), salvation within Acts is found always within believer-space ... salvation in Acts can be said to be "believer-space"' (Sleeman, 2009, p. 259).

12

Finding the Missing Ending: The Ascension for Twenty-first-century Christians

Down a single-track road with a foot-wide growth of grass in the middle of the lane, at the homestead of Caherlehillan on the Iveragh Peninsular of Kerry, in the far southwest of the Republic of Ireland, are the remains of a fifth-century church. This surely is the end of the earth, as far as someone in Roman-period Israel is concerned.

This site has evidence of the oldest known church in Ireland. To this day you can see two inscribed stones, one with a simple cross, with a scrolled ends to each arm and the top, the other with a bird sitting above a cross in a ring on a stick, with two wavy lines coming from the place where the circle meets the stick. This latter has been interpreted as a flabellum, a liturgical fan, used in worship in the early Church in the eastern Mediterranean (Sheehan, 2009). The bird is probably meant to be a peacock, a symbol of eternal life in the eastern Church of the Byzantine period,

To the early Christians being hounded out of Jerusalem, the idea of the Church actually getting to the ends of the earth may have seemed almost unbelievable, but it did.

The Church in the twenty-first century also faces challenges. In western Europe and in North America, attendance is in decline. The story of church growth that we grew up with is clearly for us no longer true; the Church is not the triumphant institution on earth we once thought it to be. So like generations before us we look to the Scriptures for insights into our faith and what it is for us in this century. Just as previous generations have thought about the Ascension and what it meant for them in their situation, what does it say to us today?

A true prophet

Back to that field in Ireland. When Luke writes that Jesus said, 'But you will receive power when the Holy Spirit has come upon you, and you will be my witnesses in Jerusalem, in all Judea and Samaria, and to the ends of the earth' (Acts 1.8), he is recording a prophecy that Jesus made. A prophecy that by the fifth century had proved to be true. As travel has improved and people from the former Roman Empire have discovered the true nature of the globe on which we live, so too has the message of Jesus travelled to the ends of the earth.

Jesus' final words about what would happen after his time on earth have come true. This vindicates him as a teacher from God. All that is recorded of what he taught in our Gospels come with the confidence that when he said something would happen it did happen. The very presence of churches in villages up and down this country and across the world is witness to the truth of Jesus' teaching.

Jesus is Lord

When Peter spoke to the gathered crowd on the Day of Pentecost about the coming of the Holy Spirit he saw it as evidence that God had made Jesus, ascended and exalted in his presence, both Lord and Messiah. He and the other disciples quickly faced persecution and hardship, but the evidence of the Ascension and the presence of the Holy Spirit gave them unshakable faith that Jesus is Lord and Messiah. In the West we do not face the same issues as they did, but life still feels challenging. So it is important for us to continue to worship the ascended Jesus as Lord, and find in him our hope.

A Church of all nations

But as well as vindicating Jesus as one sent from God, the Ascension and the fulfilment of Jesus' last words, that his followers would be his witnesses to the ends of the earth, show that a Church of all nations is God's intention. The coming of the Holy Spirit at Pentecost, giving the disciples the ability to speak in many languages, also points to this. This is reinforced by the vision that John the Divine had of the worship of God and the ascended Jesus in heaven.

> After this I looked, and there was a great multitude that no one could count, from every nation, from all tribes and peoples and languages, standing before the throne and before the Lamb, robed in white, with palm branches in their hands. They cried out in a loud voice, saying,
> 'Salvation belongs to our God who is seated on the throne, and to the Lamb!' (Revelation 7.9–10)

No longer is one nation God's people. People from all nations are part of the Church, Christ's body on earth, and this is mirrored in heaven by the worship of the Church of all nations. By the fourth century this could be seen to be a reality on earth as people from Britain to Asia were worshipping God in three persons, as followers of Jesus Christ.

Today, to continue to aspire to this vision of heaven, the Church on earth, with all her divisions and faults, needs to be what she is, a Church where people from all nations are welcomed, play their part, lead and serve. This is true for the international relationship of churches and also for churches in countries where there has been significant immigration. The voices from other nations are a gift to the Church in the country to which people have come. The Church can be more nearly what God calls it to be as it values the voices of all the nations in its midst.

The salvation journey complete

After giving the prophecy of the witness of the Church, 'as they were watching, he was lifted up, and a cloud took him out of their sight' (Acts 1.9). As we saw in Chapter 7, the Ascension is the glorification of Jesus as human and God. Our humanity, in Jesus' ascended humanity, is in the place where God is most completely known and has been accepted by God. It is this that completes the journey of salvation, which was in the mind of God before creation, and which broke into history decisively when Jesus was conceived in Mary's womb.

We are confident that God accepts us when we come to him as part of Jesus' body on earth. He accepts us just as we are as fragile, fallible, earthy creatures, and by his joining us in baptism to Jesus, we are already accepted into heaven.

In Philippians 2.6–11, Paul speaks of Jesus' descent to our humanity, and his exaltation and the confidence that every knee will bow to Jesus and acknowledge that he is Lord, to the glory of God the Father. This glorification of Jesus has happened now, people are bowing to him now. While we may wait for the day when *every* knee will bow, we can rejoice that throughout the world there are many, many worshipping today.

God and humanity reconciled

Today people still wonder if they are good enough for God. The confidence of the early Church was that in Jesus God came to our place, to the physical material world, and in Jesus' Ascension took humanity into God's place, wherever that may be, beyond our physical universe. Our fragile humanity has been fully united with God in Jesus, and he is the beginning of this new way of relating to God for humans. As John Chrysostom wrote, 'and today is the foundation of these benefits [i.e., our reconciliation with God], for as he assumed the first fruits of our nature, so He took them up to the Lord.' We don't have to strive to be good enough for God; we only need to be in Christ, to be part of who he is, to know we are accepted by God. We can relax and listen for the prompting of the Holy Spirit as to how to live out in this life our reconciliation with God.

The Head of the Church at God's right hand

The Church is the body of Christ, who is her Head: 'He is the head of the body, the church' (Colossians 1.18a). So in Jesus' Ascension there is a direct connection between the Church on earth and the Church which is in heaven. Also, after the Ascension Jesus sent his Spirit on the Church, as John records Jesus saying: '[I]f I do not go away, the Advocate will not come to you; but if I go, I will send him to you' (John 16.7) In John 14, Jesus makes it clear that the Spirit of God coming to his disciples is, in a sense, Jesus coming back to them: 'You heard me say to you, "I am going away, and I am coming to you"' (John 14.28).

So the Ascension gives us confidence that the Head of the Church, Jesus, is at God's right hand in heaven, and that he is still involved in the work of his body on earth, enlivening her by the Holy Spirit and by his intercessions (Romans 8.34; 1 John 2.1; Hebrews 7.25). This means that whatever we are doing as the body of Christ on earth, it is completely connected with what Jesus did when on earth and is still doing in heaven. So, we don't need to be anxious about what we do, nor be frozen in fear of getting things wrong. Rather, by prayer and openness to God we must let his love and power fill us and cooperate with him to 'work out our own salvation' (Philippians 2.12). As Tim Dearborn writes, 'It is not the church of God that has a mission in the world, but the God of mission who has a church in the world. The church's involvement in mission is its privileged participation in the actions of the triune God' (1997, p. 2).

The reality beyond our crises

When facing his death Stephen was granted a vision.

> But Stephen, full of the Holy Spirit, looked up to heaven and saw the glory of God, and Jesus standing at the right hand of God. 'Look,' he said, 'I see heaven open and the Son of Man standing at the right hand of God.' (Acts 7.55–56)

As he faced the ultimate crisis of his death, he was assured that Jesus was glorified, and in his place of authority. While he might be dying, yet Jesus was at God's right hand, having ascended there, exercising authority. Stephen's own death did not undermine his confidence that this was so.

The book of Revelation was written to encourage the Christians of the author's day to sense the reality behind the challenges they faced. Leon Morris puts it like this:

> John makes his point that the future belongs not to the Roman emperor, nor to any human potentate or ecclesiastic. It belongs to no man or group of men, but only to Christ, the Christ crucified for the salvation of us all. He it is who can open the book of human destiny. All of us, and the destiny of all of us are in his hands. (1988, p. 188)

Many of the historical denominations in Western Europe are facing challenges. Congregations are ageing and finances are stretched. While leadership rightly looks to what can be done to encourage evangelism and confidence in Christianity in the face of secular disdain, it risks tipping into anxious leadership. Such leadership undermines the joy of the good news that we are aiming to share. The Ascension encourages us to leave measures of 'success' to others, and to listen afresh to what the Spirit is saying to the Church, to recover our joy and confidence that Jesus is now at the right hand of God the Father and that 'neither death, nor life, nor angels, nor rulers, nor things present, nor things to come, nor powers, nor height, nor depth, nor anything else in all creation, will be able to separate us from the love of God in Christ Jesus our Lord' (Romans 8.38–39).

Bibliography

Unless otherwise referenced, quotations from ancient, medieval and early modern sources are taken from the website Early ChristianWritings.com, www.https://earlychristianwritings.com/, accessed 01.06.2024.

Barth, K., 2004, *Church Dogmatics*, Edinburgh: T&T Clark.
Beveridge, H. and Bonnet. J. eds, 1983, *Selected Works of John Calvin*, Volume 2, Michigan: Baker Book House.
Bruce, F. F., 1954, *New International Commentary on the New Testament: The Book of Acts*, Grand Rapids MI: William B. Eerdman.
Burgess, A., 2004, *The Ascension in Karl Barth*, Aldershot: Ashgate.
Davies, J. G., 1958, *He Ascended into Heaven*, London: Lutterworth Press.
Dawson, G. S., 2004, *Jesus Ascended*, London: T&T Clark.
Dearborn, T., 1997, *Beyond Duty: A Passion for Christ, a Heart for Mission*, s.l.:MARC.
Donne, B., 1983, *Christ Ascended*, Carlisle: Paternoster Press.
Edwards, D., 1976, 'Rudolf Bultmann: Scholar of Faith', *Christian Century*, September 1–8, pp. 728–30. Available online at https://www.religion-online.org/article/rudolf-bultmann-scholar-of-faith, accessed 14.06.2024.
Edwards, D., 1997, *Christianity, The First Two Thousand Years*, London: Cassell.
Farrow, D., 1999, *Ascension and Ecclesia*, Edinburgh: T&T Clark.
Fitzmeyer, J. A., 1984, 'The Ascension of Christ and Pentecost', *Theological Studies*, Volume 45, pp. 409–40.
Franklin, E., 1970, 'The Ascension and Eschatology of Acts', *Scottish Journal of Theology*, 23(3), pp. 191–200.
Kierkegaard, S., trans. H. Hong and E. Hong, 1992, *The Concluding Unscientific Postscript to 'Philosophical Fragments'*, Princeton NJ: Princeton University Press.
Martensen, H. t. U. W., 1874, *Christian Dogmatics*, Edinburgh: T&T Clark.
Morris, L., 1988, *Luke*, Tyndale Commentary, Leicester: IVP.

Ramsay, A., 1951, 'What was the Ascension?', *Bulletin of the Societas Studoriorum Novi Testamentum*, Volume 2, pp. 45–50.

Robinson, D. C., 2009, 'Informed Worship and Empowered Mission: The Integration of Liturgy, Doctrine and Praxis in Leo the Great's Sermons on Ascension and Pentecost', WORSHIP, volume 83, Number 6, November, pp. 524–40.

Sheehan, J., 2009, 'The Peacock's Tale: excavations at Caherlehillan, Kerry, Ireland', *Society for Medieval Archaeology Monographs*, Volume 21.

Sleeman, M., 2009, *Geography and the Ascension Narrative in Acts*, s.l.: Society for New Testament Studies Monograph 146.

Strelan, R., 2004, *Strange Acts: Studies in the Cultural World of the Acts of the Apostles*, Berlin: Walter de Gruyter.

Talbert, C. H., 1974, *Literary Patterns, Theological Themes and the Genre of Luke Acts*, Society of Biblical Literature Monograph Series, Volume 20.

Thompson, K., 1964, *Received up in to Glory*, London: The Faith Press.

Torrance, T., 1998, *Space, Time and Resurrection*, 2nd cdn, Edinburgh: T&T Clark.

Van Stempvoort, P., 1958/9, 'The Interpretation of the Ascension in Luke and Acts', *NTS*, Volume 5, pp. 30–42.

Williams, R., 1994, *Open to Judgement: Sermons and Addresses*, London: Darton, Longman and Todd.

Williams, R., 2007, *Tokens of Trust*, Norwich: Canterbury Press.

Zweip, A., 1997, The Ascension of the Messiah in Lukan Christology. *Supplements to Novum Testamentum*, Volume 87.

Index of Bible References

Genesis 5   14
Genesis 14   48
Genesis 28.12   48

Exodus 2.7   69
Exodus 2.23   19
Exodus 16   70
Exodus 19.9   59
Exodus 30   70
Exodus 30.10   70
Exodus 30.30   69
Exodus 40.13, 15   69
Exodus 40.34   59, 69
Exodus 40.36, 37   19

Leviticus 4   69
Leviticus 16   70
Leviticus 19.23, 24   100

Numbers 9.17, 21   19

Deuteronomy 34   25

Joshua 2.8   19

Judges 13.30   19

1 Samuel 10.1   69
1 Samuel 16.13   69

2 Samuel 2.1   69
2 Samuel 7.14   47
2 Samuel 15.30   19

2 Kings 2   15

2 Kings 20.8   19
2 Kings 23.2   19

1 Chronicles 17.13   47

2 Chronicles 5.14   59
2 Chronicles 10.18   19
2 Chronicles 29.20   19

Psalm 2.7   47
Psalm 8   47
Psalm 18.50   69
Psalm 20.6   69
Psalm 24   15, 19, 83, 97, 98
Psalm 45.6, 7   47
Psalm 47   15, 16, 19, 97
Psalm 68   15, 17, 19, 35, 66, 83
Psalm 90.4   55
Psalm 105.15   69
Psalm 110   15, 16, 83
Psalm 110.1   38, 47, 82

Isaiah 38.22   19
Isaiah 61.1   69

Daniel 7   17, 18, 30, 31, 45, 51, 52, 59
Daniel 7.9   45
Daniel 7.14   31

Micah 4.2   19

Ecclesiasticus 48   21

1 Enoch 62   22

The Missing Ending

Tobit 12 20

Matthew 3.16-17 29
Matthew 5.14 95
Matthew 25 30
Matthew 26.63-63 30
Matthew 28.16-20 31, 53

Mark 1.10 29
Mark 16.8 32
Mark 16.19 32, 132

Luke 9.28-36 23
Luke 9.51 25, 53, 117, 128, 135
Luke 24.22 129
Luke 24.26 51, 129, 130
Luke 24.31 58
Luke 24.40-53 9
Luke 24.50-53 3, 52, 133
Luke 24.51 6
Luke 24.52 6

John 3 26, 88
John 3.10-15 27
John 3.13 58, 101
John 4.21-24 57
John 6 27
John 6.62 58
John 11 74
John 11.24 39
John 14.2 107
John 14.2-3 71
John 14.28 143
John 16 28-9, 51, 72, 75, 143
John 16.7 143
John 20 12, 28-9, 51, 98

Acts 1.1-12 9
Acts 1.3 56
Acts 1.6 137-8
Acts 1.6-11 3, 7, 138
Acts 1.6-12 23, 55
Acts 1.8 55, 137, 140
Acts 1.9 56, 142

Acts 1.11 60
Acts 1.12 11, 25
Acts 2 62
Acts 2.32-36 62
Acts 2.33 72, 75
Acts 2.36 93
Acts 3 63
Acts 7.55 5
Acts 7.55-56 63, 68, 144
Acts 9 33
Acts 9.5 37
Acts 13.24 25
Acts 13.31 12
Acts 17.31 66

Romans 8.34 38, 143
Romans 8.38-39 144
Romans 10.6-7 41
Romans 10.9 64

1 Corinthians 12.3b 36
1 Corinthians 15 34
1 Corinthians 15.5-8 33
1 Corinthians 15.23-25 39
1 Corinthians 15.25-6 65

2 Corinthians 1.22 76
2 Corinthians 5.5 76

Galatians 1.14 34
Galatians 1.15-16 34
Galatians 1.16 33

Ephesians 1.20-23 39
Ephesians 4.7-10 35, 66
Ephesians 4.8, 11-12 75
Ephesians 4.9-10 69
Ephesians 4.10 69, 123

Philippians 2 73
Philippians 2.6-11 35, 142
Philippians 2.7-9 63
Philippians 2.9 92
Philippians 2.9-11 63
Philippians 2.12 143

Index of Bible References

Philippians 3.8–11   129
Philippians 3.14, 20–21   41

Colossians 1.18a   143
Colossians 3.1   40
Colossians 3.1–2   77
Colossians 3.1–4   65

1 Thessalonians 1.10   42
1 Thessalonians 4.16   42

1 Timothy 3.16   37, 129

Hebrews 1   47, 48
Hebrews 1.3   70
Hebrews 2   47
Hebrews 4   47
Hebrews 4.14–16   48
Hebrews 5.9–10   48
Hebrews 7.1–3   48
Hebrews 7.24–25   71
Hebrews 7.25   143
Hebrews 9.11–12   70
Hebrews 9.14   48
Hebrews 9.15   71

Hebrews 9.24   49
Hebrews 10.12–13   49
Hebrews 10.19–20   71
Hebrews 10.19–22   76
Hebrews 10.19–24   49
Hebrews 11   49
Hebrews 13.10   50
Hebrews 13.15–16   50

1 Peter 3.8–10   73
1 Peter 3.18–20   73
1 Peter 3.21–22   44, 67

1 John 2.1   143
1 John 3.2   68, 123

Jude 9   25

Revelation 1.5   45
Revelation 1.12–16   45
Revelation 3.21   45
Revelation 5.12–13   46
Revelation 7.9–10   141
Revelation 11   46
Revelation 12.5–6   45

Index of Authors

Aelred 106
Ambrose of Milan 96
Aquinas, Thomas 107
Aristides 81
Athanasius 92–4
Augustine of Hippo 79, 101–3

Barnabas 80, 81, 132
Barth, Karl 69, 120–1
Bede 105
Bruce, F. F. 59
Bultmann, Rudolf 118–19

Calvin, John 59, 110–11
Chrysostom, John 60, 67, 79, 98–101
Codex Bezae 4
Conzelmann, Hans 124
Cyril of Jerusalem 96–7
Cyprian 88–9

Davies, J. G. 47, 65, 122–3
Dawson, Gerrit Scott 58

Eusebius of Caesarea 94

Farrow, Douglas 103
Fitzmeyer, Joseph A. 129–30
Franklin, Eric 126

Gregory of Nazianzus 97
Gregory of Nyssa 79, 98–9

Hilary of Poitiers 94–6

Hippolytus 87–8

Ignatius 80
Irenaeus 67, 68, 83–5

Justin Martyr 81–3

Kierkegaard, Søren 114

Leo the Great 103–5
Lohfink, G. 127
Luther, Martin 110

Martensen, Hans 115–16
Methodius 90

Novatian 88

Origen 89–90, 91, 94

Parsons, M. C. 132–4
Peter of Blois 106

Ramsey, Michael 119–20

Schleiermacher, Friedrich 113
Sleeman, M. 136–8
Strauss, D. F. 115
Strelan, R. 135

Talbert, C. H. 128
Tertullian 85–7, 101
Theophanis 106
Thomas Aquinas 107–8

Torrance, T. F. 130–2

Van Stempvoort, P. A. 124–5
von Harnack, Adolf 117–18, 122

Williams, Rowan 54, 134–5

Zweip, A. 135
Zwingli, Ulrich 112

www.ingramcontent.com/pod-product-compliance
Lightning Source LLC
Chambersburg PA
CBHW060609080526
44585CB00013B/753